THE AUSTRALIAN
Women's Weekly

The
Gluten-free
Cookbook

acp
books

contents

food for thought

If you have an allergy or food sensitivity in the family, the thought of living without warm crusty bread rolls, mouth-watering muffins and scrumptious slices can be devastating.

Certainly in decades past, allergy-free baking has not been everyone's cup of carrot juice. Just the mention of 'gluten-free' conjured up images of cakes that felt like stone and tasted like cardboard.

We could only lament those poor, allergy-prone children, eating odd, uninspiring meals in the far corner of the playground, or being tragically ushered away from the birthday cake.

And pity the poor mothers who spent their lives peering, probing and poring over every morsel of food within an inch of its life – all in case a trace of nut may be lurking.

The bad news is that allergies may only get worse with global warming, as hotter, drier conditions set up our bodies for heightened immune reactions.

It's possible too that some behavioural problems in children may be linked to diet, particularly sensitivity to food chemicals and gluten.

For the modern mum and dad, this means rather than a food allergy being a rare occurrence, you can expect at least two or three of the children you'll invite to your child's birthday party to have some sort of food sensitivity or allergy.

The good news is there's plenty you can do about it, and whether you're cooking for allergies in your own family, or simply have the social smarts and good conscience to make a gluten-free birthday cake for your child's friends, we've covered all bases with the recipes in this book.

what is Coeliac Disease?

Despite a common misconception, Coeliac Disease is not actually an allergy, but rather an auto-immune disease, that causes damage to the lining of the small intestine when gluten is consumed. Just as people with nut allergies avoid nuts, the only way to treat Coeliac Disease is to avoid wheat, rye, barley and oat products. Coeliac Disease is diagnosed by a blood screening test (tissue transglutaminase) that a GP can arrange, followed by a small bowel biopsy by a gastroenterologist to confirm it. Coeliac Disease should not be confused with wheat allergy, which rarely occurs beyond infancy, or the stomach and bowel irritation that gluten can sometimes cause in people with chemical intolerances, who may also benefit from a gluten-free diet.

There is much variability in the severity of Coeliac Disease with relatively mild to quite severe symptoms listed below. If you have Coeliac Disease, it's not a case of a little gluten every now and then won't hurt. It's essential that you maintain a strict gluten-free diet. While some foods like wheat, rye and barley have to be strictly avoided, other foods such as pure, uncontaminated oats are tolerated by some people with Coeliac Disease, but not by others – to be on the safe side, oats are best avoided completely. To take the agony out of your shopping, we have provided a list of foods that are safe to eat for anyone on a gluten-free diet. While this list is not complete, it certainly gives you a good indication of foods that should be avoided.

spotting the symptoms of Coeliac Disease

The symptoms of Coeliac Disease include fatigue, lack of energy, low iron levels, unusual or excessive wind or burping, feeling full after only a small amount of food, bloating, stomach cramps, diarrhoea, poor weight gain or delayed growth, or sometimes weight gain. Less common symptoms include bruising easily, mouth ulcers, depression, dental problems, miscarriages and joint and bone

problems. People with Coeliac Disease tend to be more likely to be at risk of osteoporosis because of poor absorption of nutrients to the bones. Coeliac Disease also tends to be a multi-system disorder and can often go hand in hand with other auto-immune diseases especially type 1 Diabetes, thyroid problems and a severe skin condition called Dermatitis Herpitiformis.

the gluten-free diet

Living and eating with gluten intolerance or allergy doesn't have to be fiddly or expensive, if you know a few shortcuts. Here are our top tips for gluten-free baking:

• Don't waste a flop just because you're cooking gluten-free. If your fruitcake or mud cake is a disaster, break it up, mix with a little alcohol and dip in melted chocolate for delicious truffles. Save all stale/unused bread for meatloaf, stuffing, casserole toppings etc. If cookies fall apart, crumble them in layers with yogurt or make a trifle out of them. You can also use them as a base for a slice or cheesecake.

• Be precise. Keep measuring cups for dry ingredients and a measuring jug for wet. Being exact is an important rule for any baking, but even more so in gluten-free cooking as gluten is the very element in wheat flour that holds things together and gives baked goods their spring.

In gluten-free cooking, there's a lot of chemical science involved as you are often using more than one flour, each of a different texture and consistency. Rice flour for instance is gritty, while soy flour is finer. The good news is that we've done the hard work for you in the Test Kitchen to work out exactly the right ratios. So measure precisely and use the flours prescribed rather than taking the 'any old flour will do' approach. And always be sure to use a spatula to level off the top and flatten the surface to achieve the most accurate measurement with dry ingredients.

• Beware of some labels – not all foods are what they seem. Most cornflakes for instance contain malt extract (barley), while icing sugar mixture may contain wheat. We use pure icing sugar instead, which contains only sugar.

• Always cover gluten-free baked goods as they can dry out quickly.

• Find a gluten-free or allergy-free cooking buddy. Trying things is much more fun when you can find a kindred spirit.

• Store, label and use gluten-free flours and non gluten-free flours separately to avoid contamination.

• Pastry and biscuit dough is easier to handle if refrigerated.

• After baking cakes, slices, muffins, etc, wrap and freeze them. Wrapping items individually allows you to use just what is required.

• Oven temperature is important in the baking of gluten-free foods. If you are having ongoing problems with gluten-free baking, check your oven temperature. Oven thermometers can be purchased from a kitchenware shop.

what you can eat

If you have Coeliac Disease or a gluten sensitivity these are the foods you can eat:

• All fresh fruit and vegetables.

• Dairy. Milk, cream, cheese, most yogurts, butter, margarine, cottage cheese, sour cream, most ice-creams (check labels for an ingredient from a gluten source, or cake or biscuit bits). Glucose syrup from wheat is gluten-free and OK even though it sounds like it isn't.

• Beef, pork, lamb, poultry, veal, fish and shellfish, eggs, dried beans, peas, tofu, plain nuts and peanut butter.

- Check ingredients on all manufactured or pressed meats and other smallgoods.
- Products labelled gluten-free in Australia (in some other countries some gluten is allowed in products labelled gluten-free).
- Oils, butter and margarine.
- Herbs and most spices (but check labels for wheat as an ingredient).
- All alcohol except beer (though gluten-free beers are now available).
- Plain rice cakes, rice crackers, popcorn, plain potato and corn chips.
- Canned tuna, chicken, canned beans and lentils, some spaghetti sauces (check labels).
- Beverages like fruit juices, instant and ground coffee, tea, soft drinks.

did you know?
Check labels when choosing lollies – glucose syrup made from wheat is actually gluten-free.

- Check labels on all condiments such as mustard, ketchup, horseradish and jellies, relish, pickles, olives and vanilla.
- Sugar, honey, salt and pepper.
- Rice and corn cereals without malt extract (barley), rice puffs, rice bran, buckwheat puffs, millet puffs, amaranth, sorghum, gluten-free muesli, rice porridge, psyllium husks.
- Gluten-free pasta, rice noodles or vermicelli.
- Gluten-free stock and gravy are now available.

what you can't eat

If you have Coeliac Disease or a gluten sensitivity these are the foods you need to avoid:

- Avoid wheat, barley, rye, farina, graham flour, semolina, durum, atta, bulgar, kamut, kasha, matzo meal, spelt, triticale, malt (from barley), malt extract (from barley) and oats (while oats affect some people with Coeliac Disease but not others, it is best avoided completely).
- Remember most processed foods from grains contain gluten. Avoid these foods unless they're labelled as gluten-free or made with corn, rice, soy or other gluten-free grain. These foods include: breads, cereals, crackers, croutons, pasta and cookies, cakes and pies.
- Check ingredients on other processed foods such as soups, gravies, sauces (including soy sauce), many lollies, imitation meat or seafood, processed luncheon meats, self-basting poultry.
- Food additives such as thickeners and starches made from wheat.
- Medications and vitamins that use wheat starch as a binding agent.
- Playdough, made from wheat flour – young children often eat playdough when they play with it, so be alert if your child has Coeliac Disease.

Source: The Coeliac Society of Australia

other food allergies

Food allergies differ from one person to the next. While for one person eating egg or drinking milk may cause bowel symptoms or skin rashes, those who are highly allergic may have a life-threatening reaction that can stop them breathing.

spotting the symptoms

The symptoms of food allergies can range from most commonly hives and eczema to less commonly low blood pressure, dizziness or faintness. Swelling of the lips and throat which in severe cases can cause difficulty breathing (anaphylaxis) is a rare, but life-threatening symptom. Other common food allergy signs include diarrhoea, vomiting, dry, itchy throat and tongue, coughing, wheezing and a runny or blocked nose.

top tip

If planning to dine at a restaurant, it is a good idea to phone in advance. This way you can learn what is on the menu, ask about ingredients and explain what you cannot eat. If you are not confident about getting a gluten-free meal after speaking to the restaurant, it would be wise to go elsewhere.

what you can't eat

Foods that may be detrimental for people with egg, nut and dairy allergies include the following:

- **egg:** For those who have an egg allergy remember to watch out for the presence of eggs in foods where labels mention albumin, egg solids, egg substitutes, eggnog, globulin, livetin, lysozyme, mayonnaise, meringue, ovalbumin, ovamucin, ovmucoid, ovovilen and vitellen. Watch ice-creams, custards, soups and many decadent desserts like soufflé, tiramisu and crème caramel.

- **nuts:** People with nut and seed allergies should always read labels for traces of nuts or sesame. Apart from the obvious like peanut butter, nuts can also be in nougat or marzipan, chocolates and cakes, crackers, cereals and other baked goods. Even some shampoos have traces of sesame seed, poppy seed and cotton seed that can lead to itchiness or even severe reactions for some people. For people allergic to sesame don't forget common culprits like hummus, stir-fries and chutney. And of course tahini, bagels, bread sticks and vegie burgers.

• **dairy:** And if it's dairy that you're allergic to or if you have lactose intolerance? Remember cow's milk is not only found in butter, cream, milk and cheese among other dairy foods, but is also disguised on labels as whey, casein, hydrosalates (casein, milk protein, whey and whey protein), caseinates (calcium, ammonium, magnesium, potassium, sodium). Other culprits are lactalbumin, lactoglobulin, lactose and Opta (fat substitute). Speak to your doctor about other ways to get enough calcium in your diet.

menu tips

Home is covered but what about dining out? Here are some hidden terms for gluten that you need to watch for:
• Au gratin – a topping of breadcrumbs and cheese.
• Béchamel – white sauce made by thickening milk with a butter and flour mixture.
• Cordon bleu – chicken or veal dish with ham and cheese which is crumbed (breadcrumbs) and fried.
• Encrusted – may use flour or breadcrumbs to bind ingredients.
• Dusted – sprinkled with flour.
• Farfel – a soup garnish made of minced noodle dough.
• Marinade – this may contain soy sauce.

Note: These lists are not exhaustive. For further advice consult your allergist.

food intolerances

Food intolerances are not the same as a food allergy. An intolerance means you may experience an adverse reaction to certain foods, but this does not involve the immune system. You can also generally tolerate a little of these foods before you experience symptoms such as stomach and bowel upsets, bloating, hives and headaches. While the symptoms can be unpleasant they are generally not life threatening. Comprehensive assessment by an allergist/immunologist can help determine the type of allergy or intolerance.

In *The Gluten-free Cookbook* we understand that you're committed to good health, a household budget and fuss-free cooking.

Of the 50 mouth-watering recipes in this book, all are wheat flour-free for gluten-sensitive folks, while others are specifically tailored for people with life-threatening nut allergies, or for people with the itchy and scratchy life that goes with an egg or dairy allergy. Just follow the key at the beginning of the recipe to ensure you're cooking for your allergy condition (gluten-free, wheat-free, yeast-free, dairy-free, egg-free or nut-free). All ingredients are available in supermarkets and health food stores.

breakfast

These five delicious recipes for both weekday and weekend breakfasts are a surprise and a delight. Who would have thought allergy-free food could taste so good?

waffles with maple syrup

This recipe is gluten-free, wheat-free, yeast-free and dairy-free.

1 Beat spread, caster sugar and extract in medium bowl with electric mixer until light and fluffy. Beat in egg yolks one at a time.
2 Beat egg whites in small bowl with electric mixer until soft peaks form, fold into egg yolk mixture.
3 Fold in sifted dry ingredients and water. Do not overmix. Mixture may look slightly curdled.
4 Spray heated waffle iron with cooking oil; pour ½ cup batter over bottom element of waffle iron. Close iron; cook waffle about 3 minutes or until browned both sides and crisp. Transfer waffle to plate; cover to keep warm. Repeat with cooking oil spray and remaining batter.
5 Serve waffles dusted with sifted icing sugar and maple syrup.
prep + cook time 45 minutes **makes** 12
nutritional count per waffle 15.8g total fat (2.9g saturated fat); 1622kJ (388 cal); 58.1g carbohydrate; 3g protein; 0.8g fibre
storage Waffles can be frozen in an airtight container for up to 3 months. Reheat waffles in the oven.

200g dairy-free spread
¾ cup (165g) caster sugar
1 teaspoon vanilla extract
3 eggs, separated
1¼ cups (185g) potato flour
1 cup (200g) brown rice flour
1 teaspoon gluten-free
    baking powder
1 cup (250ml) water
cooking-oil spray
2 teaspoons pure icing sugar
1 cup (250ml) pure maple syrup

toasted muesli

This recipe is gluten-free, wheat-free, yeast-free and egg-free.

2 tablespoons golden syrup
2 tablespoons macadamia oil
1 cup (50g) gluten-free
  cornflakes
1 cup (110g) rolled rice
1 cup (20g) puffed rice
1 cup (140g) coarsely
  chopped macadamias
1 cup (140g) coarsely
  chopped pistachios
1 cup (160g) coarsely
  chopped almond kernels
½ cup (25g) flaked coconut
½ cup (100g) finely chopped
  dried figs
½ cup (65g) dried cranberries

1 Preheat oven to 180°C/160°C fan-forced.
2 Combine syrup and oil in small bowl.
3 Combine cornflakes, rolled rice, puffed rice, nuts and coconut in shallow baking dish; drizzle with syrup mixture. Roast, uncovered, about 15 minutes or until browned lightly, stirring halfway through roasting time. Cool 10 minutes.
4 Stir fruit into muesli mixture; cool.

prep + cook time 25 minutes (+ cooling)
makes 8 cups or **serves** 24 (⅓ cup per serve)
nutritional count per serving 2.7g total fat (2.1g saturated fat); 811kJ (194 cal); 13.5g carbohydrate; 3.7g protein; 2.7g fibre
storage Store muesli in an airtight container in the refrigerator for up to one month.

apple + ricotta fritters

This recipe is gluten-free, wheat-free and yeast-free.

. . . .

1 Combine ricotta, sifted flour, sugar, nutmeg, egg and apple in medium bowl.

2 Heat oil in large saucepan; deep-fry rounded tablespoons of ricotta mixture, in batches, until browned lightly. Drain on absorbent paper. Toss fritters in combined extra sugar and cinnamon.

3 Serve fritters drizzled with maple syrup.

prep + cook time 25 minutes **makes** 24

nutritional count per fritter 3.8g total fat (1.5g saturated fat); 355kJ (85 cal); 10.3g carbohydrate; 2.2g protein; 0.2g fibre

1¾ cups (420g) ricotta cheese

⅔ cup (90g) gluten-free
   self-raising flour

2 tablespoons caster sugar

½ teaspoon ground nutmeg

1 egg

1 large apple (200g), peeled,
   chopped finely

vegetable oil, for deep-frying

⅓ cup (75g) caster sugar, extra

1 teaspoon ground cinnamon

2 tablespoons pure maple syrup

rolled rice porridge

This recipe is gluten-free, wheat-free, yeast-free, dairy-free, egg-free and nut-free.

1½ cups (160g) rolled rice
1.125 litres (4½ cups) water
⅓ cup (80ml) rice milk
⅓ cup (50g) coarsely chopped
  dried apricots
¼ cup (10g) flaked coconut,
  toasted
2 tablespoons honey

1 Combine rolled rice and 3 cups of the water in medium bowl. Cover; stand at room temperature overnight.

2 Place undrained rolled rice in medium saucepan; cook, stirring, until mixture comes to the boil. Add the remaining water; bring to the boil. Reduce heat; simmer, uncovered, for about 5 minutes or until thickened.

3 Divide porridge and milk among serving bowls. Sprinkle with apricots and coconut; drizzle with honey.

prep + cook time 20 minutes (+ standing) **serves** 4
nutritional count per serving 2.8g total fat (1.7g saturated fat); 1053kJ (252 cal); 50.7g carbohydrate; 3.9g protein; 2.7g fibre
tip You can substitute the rice milk for soy, whole or skim milk.

banana hotcakes

This recipe is gluten-free, wheat-free, yeast-free and nut-free.

. . . .

1 Sift flours and sugar into medium bowl. Whisk milk, eggs and half the butter in medium jug. Gradually whisk milk mixture into flour mixture until smooth.

2 Heat large heavy-based frying pan over medium heat; brush with a little of the remaining butter. Pour 2 tablespoons batter for each pancake into heated pan (you can cook three at a time). Cook pancakes until bubbles appear on the surface; top pancakes with banana, sprinkle each pancake with a rounded teaspoon of brown sugar. Turn pancakes, cook until sugar has caramelised and banana is browned lightly. Cover to keep warm.

3 Repeat process using remaining melted butter, batter, banana and brown sugar, wiping out pan between batches.

prep + cook time 25 minutes **makes** 12

nutritional count per hotcake 5.1g total fat (2.8g saturated fat); 748kJ (179 cal); 29.3g carbohydrate; 3.3g protein; 0.9g fibre

goes well with extra fresh sliced banana and maple syrup.

1¼ cups (175g) gluten-free
   self-raising flour
¼ cup (50g) brown rice flour
2 tablespoons caster sugar
1 cup (250ml) milk
3 eggs
40g butter, melted
2 large bananas (460g),
   sliced thickly
¼ cup (55g) brown sugar

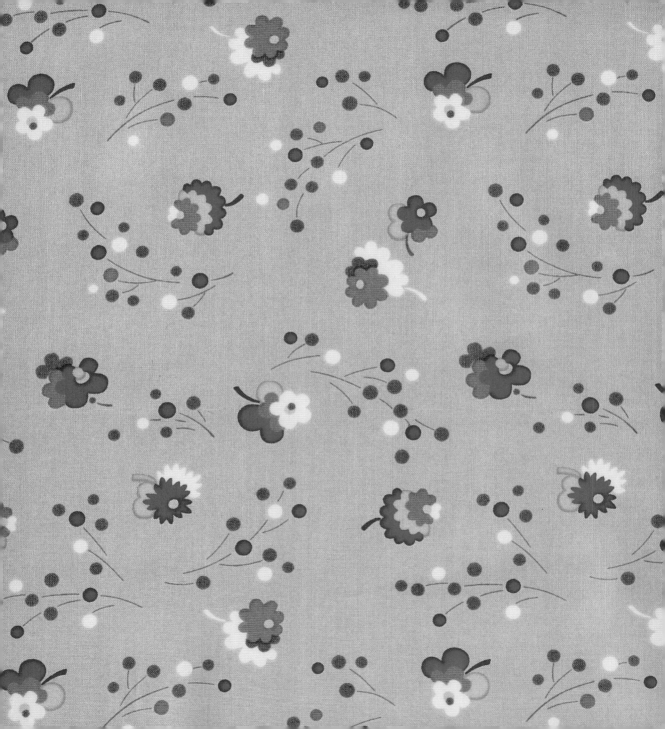

the lunchbox

Lunch, particularly when you're at work or school, presents the biggest problems when you're gluten-intolerant – no sandwiches. These delicious lunchbox solutions will make you the envy of your friends.

rice noodle cakes

This recipe is gluten-free, wheat-free, yeast-free, dairy-free and nut-free.

1 Place noodles in large heatproof bowl; cover with boiling water. Stand 5 minutes or until tender; drain. Cut noodles coarsely with scissors.

2 Combine noodles, egg, carrot, zucchini, coriander and sauce in large bowl.

3 Heat a little of the oil in large frying pan; cook ¼-cup mixture, flattening slightly with spatula, until browned both sides. Repeat with remaining oil and noodle mixture, cooking three or four cakes at a time.

4 Serve noodle cakes with extra sweet chilli sauce.

prep + cook time 35 minutes **makes** 20

nutritional count per cake 2.8g total fat (0.5g saturated fat); 263kJ (63 cal); 7.2g carbohydrate; 1.8g protein; 0.5g fibre

storage Store cooked rice noodle cakes in an airtight container in the refrigerator for up to 3 days or freeze for up to 3 months. Rice noodle cakes can be eaten cold or reheated in the microwave on HIGH (100%) for about 30 seconds.

200g rice vermicelli noodles

3 eggs, beaten lightly

1 medium carrot (120g), grated coarsely

1 medium zucchini (120g), grated coarsely

½ cup coarsely chopped fresh coriander

2 tablespoons gluten-free sweet chilli sauce

2 tablespoons vegetable oil

zucchini, olive + tomato polenta fingers

This recipe is gluten-free, wheat-free, yeast-free, egg-free and nut-free.

2 cups (500ml) water

2 cups (500ml) gluten-free chicken stock

1 cup (170g) polenta

1 large zucchini (150g), grated coarsely

½ cup (80g) coarsely chopped seeded black olives

⅓ cup (25g) finely grated parmesan cheese

¼ cup (35g) semi-dried tomatoes in oil, drained, chopped finely

2 tablespoons olive oil

1 Oil deep 19cm-square cake pan; line base and sides with baking paper.

2 Bring the water and stock to the boil in large saucepan; gradually stir in polenta. Reduce heat; simmer, stirring, about 10 minutes or until polenta thickens. Stir in zucchini, olives, cheese and tomato. Spread polenta mixture into pan; cover, refrigerate about 1 hour or until polenta is firm.

3 Turn polenta onto board; cut in half. Cut each half into six slices.

4 Heat oil in large frying pan; cook polenta, until browned both sides.

prep + cook time 25 minutes (+ refrigeration) **makes** 12

nutritional count per finger 4.5g total fat (1g saturated fat); 439kJ (105 cal); 12.7g carbohydrate; 2.9g protein; 1.1g fibre

storage Cooked polenta fingers can be stored in an airtight container in the refrigerator for up to 3 days. Polenta fingers can be eaten cold or reheated in the microwave on HIGH (100%) for 30 seconds.

omelette wrap

This recipe is gluten-free, wheat-free, yeast-free and nut-free.

. . . .

1 Spray medium frying pan with cooking oil; cook half the eggs over medium heat, swirling pan to make a thin omelette. Remove from pan; cool on baking-paper-covered wire rack. Repeat with remaining eggs.

2 Combine mayonnaise, dill and lemon juice in small bowl.

3 Spread each omelette with half of the mayonnaise mixture; top with watercress, salmon and cucumber. Roll omelette to enclose filling.

prep + cook time 15 minutes (+ cooling) **makes** 2

nutritional count per wrap 20.8 total fat (4.5g saturated fat); 1308kJ (313 cal); 5.2g carbohydrate; 25.9g protein; 1.4g fibre

tip The omelette and mayonnaise mixture can be made the night before and stored, covered, in the refrigerator until ready to assemble the next day.

cooking-oil spray

4 eggs, beaten lightly

2 tablespoons gluten-free mayonnaise

2 teaspoons finely chopped fresh dill

1 teaspoon lemon juice

100g watercress, trimmed

100g smoked salmon

½ lebanese cucumber (65g), seeded, cut into matchsticks

pizza pinwheels

This recipe is gluten-free, wheat-free, yeast-free and nut-free.

125g butter, softened

1 tablespoon pure icing sugar

2 eggs yolks

1 cup (220g) cooked mashed
potato, sieved

1 cup (150g) potato flour

½ cup (80g) brown rice flour

1 tablespoon gluten-free
baking powder

⅓ cup (90g) tomato paste

125g gluten-free shaved ham,
chopped finely

30g baby spinach leaves

1½ cups (150g) pizza cheese

1 Preheat oven to 220°C/200°C fan-forced. Oil 19cm x 29cm slice pan.

2 Beat butter, sifted sugar and yolks in small bowl with electric mixer until light and fluffy. Transfer mixture to large bowl; stir in potato.

3 Stir in sifted dry ingredients to make a soft dough. Knead dough lightly on floured surface until smooth. Roll dough between sheets of baking paper to 20cm x 30cm rectangle.

4 Spread tomato paste over dough; sprinkle with ham, spinach and 1 cup of the cheese.

5 Starting from long side, roll dough firmly, using paper as a guide; trim ends. Cut roll into 12 slices; place pinwheels, cut-side up, in single layer, in pan. Bake 20 minutes. Remove pinwheels from oven, sprinkle with remaining cheese; bake further 10 minutes.

6 Serve pinwheels warm or cold.

prep + cook time 50 minutes **makes** 12

nutritional count per pinwheel 13.4g total fat (8g saturated fat); 961kJ (230 cal); 19.7g carbohydrate; 7.4g protein; 1.1g fibre

storage Pinwheels can be stored in an airtight container in the refrigerator overnight or freezer for up to 3 months.

indian vegetable fritters

This recipe is gluten-free, wheat-free, yeast-free, egg-free and dairy-free (unless served with yogurt).

1 Using hand, combine flour, carrot, onion, peas, garlic, spices, baking powder, coriander and the water in medium bowl.
2 Heat oil in wok; deep-fry level tablespoons of vegetable mixture, in batches, until browned lightly and cooked through. Remove with a slotted spoon; drain on absorbent paper.
3 Fritters can be served with natural yogurt.

prep + cook time 45 minutes **makes** 36

nutritional count per fritter 2g total fat (0.3g saturated fat); 213kJ (51 cal); 5.8g carbohydrate; 2.2g protein; 1.6g fibre

storage Fritters can be stored in an airtight container in the refrigerator for up to 3 days. Eat cold or reheat fritters in the microwave on HIGH (100%) for about 20 seconds.

2 cups (300g) chickpea flour
2 large carrots (360g), grated coarsely
1 large brown onion (200g), sliced thinly
1 cup (120g) frozen peas
2 cloves garlic, crushed
1 teaspoon ground cumin
1 teaspoon garam masala
¼ teaspoon ground turmeric
½ teaspoon gluten-free baking powder
⅓ cup coarsely chopped fresh coriander
¼ cup (60ml) water
vegetable oil, for deep-frying

potato + oregano pizza

This recipe is gluten-free, wheat-free, yeast-free, dairy-free and nut-free.

375g packet gluten-free
    bread mix
300g baby new potatoes,
    sliced thinly
2 teaspoons finely chopped
    fresh oregano
2 teaspoons olive oil
1 clove garlic, crushed

1 Preheat oven to 220°C/200°C fan-forced. Oil two 25cm x 35cm swiss roll pans; line bases with baking paper, extending paper 5cm over long sides.

2 Make bread mix according to packet directions; spread mixture into pans.

3 Combine remaining ingredients in medium bowl; spread potato mixture over bread mix.

4 Bake pizzas about 20 minutes or until potato is tender and bases are crisp.

prep + cook time 45 minutes **serves** 6

nutritional count per serving 2.3g total fat (0.4g saturated fat); 1116kJ (267 cal); 40.9g carbohydrate; 8.1g protein; 2.8g fibre

storage Pizza slices can be stored in an airtight container in the refrigerator for up to 2 days. Pizza slices can be eaten cold or reheated in the microwave on HIGH (100%) for about 30 seconds.

beef lasagne

This recipe is gluten-free, wheat-free, yeast-free, dairy-free, egg-free and nut-free.

. . . .

1 Heat oil in large frying pan; cook onion, celery, zucchini, carrot and garlic, stirring, until onion is soft. Add beef; cook, stirring, until changed in colour. Add undrained tomatoes and paste; cook, stirring, about 10 minutes or until sauce thickens slightly.

2 Meanwhile, make white sauce.

3 Preheat oven to 180°C/160°C fan-forced. Oil deep 10-cup capacity rectangular ovenproof dish.

4 Dip eight rice paper squares, one at a time, into bowl of warm water until soft; place on board covered with tea towel. Spread 1½ cups beef mixture over base of dish; top with softened rice paper sheets. Top with half of the remaining beef mixture and half of the white sauce.

5 Soften the remaining rice paper, place on top of beef mixture; top with remaining beef mixture and white sauce.

6 Bake lasagne, uncovered about 50 minutes or until browned lightly. Stand 10 minutes, sprinkle with chives before serving.

white sauce Combine the water, milk, cloves and bay leaf in medium saucepan; bring to the boil. Strain milk mixture into large heatproof jug; discard solids. Melt spread in same saucepan; add cornflour, cook, stirring 1 minute. Gradually add hot milk mixture, stirring constantly, until mixture boils and thickens. Stir in cheese.

prep + cook time 1 hour 30 minutes **serves** 6

nutritional count per serving 15.2g total fat (4.2g saturated fat); 1484kJ (355 cal); 26.9g carbohydrate; 25.3g protein; 4.5g fibre

tip If you do not have an intolerance to milk products you can substitute the soy milk and water in the white sauce recipe for 2½ cups (625ml) whole cows milk.

storage Lasagne can be stored in the refrigerator overnight or freezer for up to 3 months.

2 teaspoons olive oil

1 medium brown onion (150g), chopped finely

1 trimmed celery stalk (100g), chopped finely

1 small zucchini (90g), chopped finely

1 small carrot (70g), chopped finely

2 cloves garlic, crushed

600g beef mince

810g can crushed tomatoes

½ cup (140g) tomato paste

16 x 17cm rice paper squares

1 tablespoon finely chopped fresh chives

white sauce

1½ cups (375ml) water

1 cup (250ml) gluten-free soy milk

2 cloves

1 bay leaf

2 tablespoons dairy-free spread

2 tablespoons (corn) cornflour

100g chive-flavoured soy cheese, chopped coarsely

pancetta + cheese muffins

This recipe is gluten-free, wheat-free, yeast-free and nut-free.

1 teaspoon olive oil

200g gluten-free pancetta, chopped finely

4 green onions, sliced thinly

1¼ cups (175g) gluten-free self-raising flour

⅓ cup (55g) polenta

¾ cup (75g) pizza cheese

⅔ cup (160ml) milk

2 eggs

60g butter, melted

1 Preheat oven to 200°C/180°C fan-forced. Line 12-hole (⅓-cup/80ml) muffin pan with paper cases.

2 Heat oil in medium frying pan; cook pancetta, stirring, about 3 minutes or until browned lightly. Add onion; cook, stirring, until soft. Cool.

3 Combine flour, polenta and ½ cup of the cheese in medium bowl; stir in combined milk and eggs, melted butter and pancetta mixture.

4 Divide mixture among paper cases; sprinkle with remaining cheese. Bake about 20 minutes. Stand muffins in pan 5 minutes; turn, top-side up, onto wire rack to cool.

prep + cook time 35 minutes **makes** 12

nutritional count per muffin 9.7g total fat (5.1g saturated fat); 598kJ (143 cal); 16.7g carbohydrate; 7.2g protein; 0.4g fibre

storage Muffins can be stored in the refrigerator in an airtight container for up to 2 days or freezer for up to 3 months.

egg, bacon + parmesan pies

This recipe is gluten-free, wheat-free and yeast-free.

1 Make pastry.

2 Preheat oven to 220°C/200°C fan-forced. Oil 6-hole (¾-cup/180ml) texas muffin pan.

3 Roll pastry between sheets of baking paper until 5mm thick; cut six 11cm rounds from pastry. Ease pastry rounds into pan holes, press into base and sides; prick bases with fork.

4 Bake pastry cases about 10 minutes or until browned lightly. Cool cases in pan. Reduce oven temperature to 200°C/180°C fan-forced.

5 Meanwhile, heat oil in small frying pan; cook bacon, onion and garlic, stirring, until bacon is soft. Divide bacon mixture among pastry cases.

6 Whisk eggs and cream in medium jug; stir in cheese and chives. Fill pastry cases with egg mixture. Bake about 25 minutes or until set.

pastry Process flours, cheese and butter until fine. Add enough of the water to make ingredients come together. Cover; refrigerate 30 minutes.

prep + cook time 50 minutes (+ refrigeration and cooling) makes 6
nutritional count per pie 37.9g total fat (20.8g saturated fat); 2291kJ (548 cal); 54g carbohydrate; 17.6g protein; 1.5g fibre
storage Pies can be stored in an airtight container in the refrigerator for up to 3 days or freezer for up to 1 month.

2 teaspoons vegetable oil

3 rindless bacon rashers (195g), chopped finely

1 small brown onion (80g), chopped finely

1 clove garlic, crushed

4 eggs

¼ cup (60ml) cream

¼ cup (20g) finely grated parmesan cheese

1 tablespoon finely chopped fresh chives

pastry

1 cup (200g) rice flour

¼ cup (35g) (corn) cornflour

¼ cup (30g) soya flour

¼ cup (20g) finely grated parmesan cheese

150g cold butter, chopped

2 tablespoons cold water, approximately

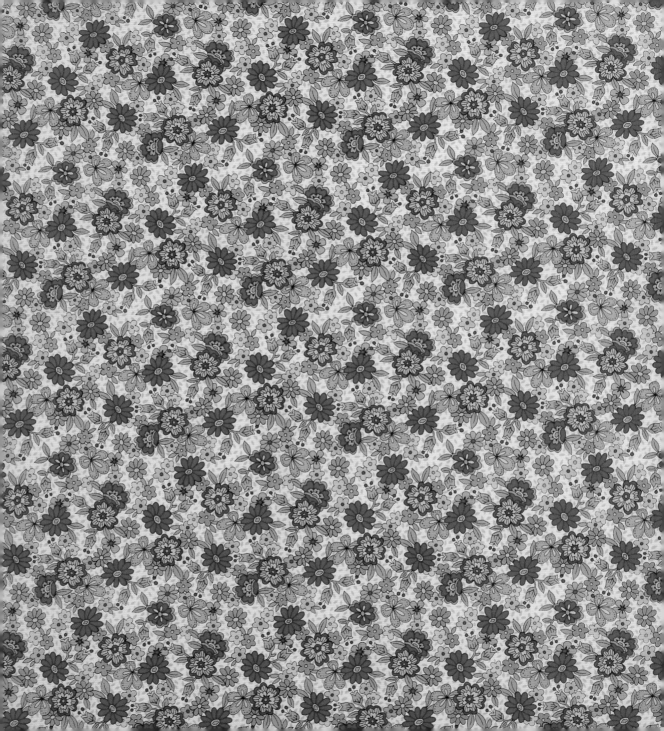

kids' parties

An allergic child can feel seriously left out at parties. These recipes for good-looking and good-tasting party food don't look in the least like 'special' food. All the party guests will be coming back for more.

mini meat pies

This recipe is gluten-free, wheat-free, yeast-free and nut-free.

2 teaspoons vegetable oil

1 medium brown onion (150g), chopped finely

2 rindless bacon rashers (130g), chopped finely

350g beef mince

2 tablespoons tomato paste

¼ cup (35g) arrowroot

2 cups (500ml) gluten-free beef stock

1 egg, beaten lightly

pastry

1¾ cups (350g) rice flour

⅓ cup (50g) (corn) cornflour

⅓ cup (40g) soya flour

200g cold butter, chopped

¼ cup (60ml) cold water, approximately

1 Heat oil in medium saucepan; cook onion and bacon, stirring, until onion softens and bacon is browned. Add beef; cook, stirring, until browned. Add paste and blended arrowroot and stock; bring to the boil stirring. Reduce heat; simmer, uncovered, until thickened. Cool.

2 Meanwhile, make pastry.

3 Preheat oven to 220°C/200°C fan-forced. Oil 12 x ¼-cup (60ml) foil pie cases (7cm diameter top, 5cm diameter base); place on oven tray.

4 Roll pastry between sheets of baking paper until 5mm thick; cut 12 x 9cm rounds from pastry. Ease pastry rounds into cases; press into base and sides. Spoon beef mixture into pastry cases; brush edges with egg. Cut 12 x 7cm rounds from remaining pastry; place rounds on pies, press to seal edges. Brush pies with egg; cut two small slits in top of each pie.

5 Bake pies about 25 minutes. Serve with gluten-free tomato sauce.

pastry Process flours and butter until mixture is fine. Add enough of the water to make ingredients come together. Cover; refrigerate 30 minutes.

prep + cook time 1 hour (+ refrigeration and standing) **makes** 12
nutritional count per pie 19.3g total fat (11g saturated fat); 1032kJ (247 cal); 7.8g carbohydrate; 10.7g protein; 0.7g fibre
storage Pies can be frozen for up to 1 month.

mini pizza squares

This recipe is gluten-free, wheat-free, yeast-free and nut-free.

. . . .

1 Preheat oven to 220°C/200°C fan-forced. Oil two 25cm x 35cm swiss roll pans; line bases with baking paper, extending paper 5cm over long sides.

2 Make bread mix according to packet directions; spread mixture into pans. Bake about 12 minutes or until browned lightly. Remove from oven.

3 Spread paste over bases. Sprinkle sliced tomato, capsicum, onion and fetta over one pizza base; sprinkle pineapple, ham and pizza cheese over remaining pizza base.

4 Bake pizzas, about 15 minutes or until cheese melts and bases are crisp. Cut each pizza into 20 squares. Top each capsicum and fetta pizza square with olives and basil leaves. Top each ham and pineapple pizza square with a cherry tomato quarter and an oregano leaf.

prep + cook time 50 minutes **makes** 40 squares (20 of each pizza)

nutritional count per capsicum and fetta pizza square
2.5g total fat (1.2g saturated fat); 284kJ (68 cal); 8.3g carbohydrate; 2.8g protein; 0.7g fibre

nutritional count per ham and pineapple pizza square
1.4g total fat (0.8g saturated fat); 272kJ (65 cal); 9.1g carbohydrate; 3.6g protein; 0.8g fibre

375g packet gluten-free
  bread mix
⅓ cup (90g) tomato paste
2 medium tomatoes (300g),
  sliced thinly
270g jar char-grilled capsicum in
  oil, drained, chopped coarsely
½ small red onion (50g),
  sliced thinly
150g soft fetta cheese, crumbled
440g can pineapple pieces,
  drained
100g shaved gluten-free ham,
  chopped coarsely
1 cup (100g) pizza cheese
½ cup (60g) seeded green
  olives, halved
20 small fresh basil leaves
5 cherry tomatoes (100g),
  quartered
20 fresh oregano leaves

crunchy chicken fingers

This recipe is gluten-free, wheat-free, yeast-free, dairy-free and nut-free.

8 chicken tenderloins (600g)

100g packet gluten-free
   plain potato crisps

1 egg white

⅓ cup (80ml) gluten-free
   sweet chilli sauce

1 Preheat oven to 200°C/180°C fan-forced.

2 Cut tenderloins in half, diagonally.

3 Crush chips coarsely, while still in the bag, place in medium shallow bowl. Whisk egg white lightly in small shallow bowl.

4 Dip chicken pieces in egg white then in chips to coat; place in single layer, on oiled wire rack over oven tray.

5 Bake chicken fingers about 15 minutes or until chicken is cooked through. Serve fingers with sauce.

prep + cook time 30 minutes **makes** 16

nutritional count per finger 4.2g total fat (1.5g saturated fat); 376kJ (90 cal); 4g carbohydrate; 8.7g protein; 1g fibre

tip Tomato sauce can be substituted for sweet chilli sauce.

storage Leftover chicken fingers can be kept in the refrigerator for 1 day, and reheated in the oven.

mini corn + chive muffins

This recipe is gluten-free, wheat-free, yeast-free and nut-free.

. . . .

1 Preheat oven to 200°C/180°C fan-forced. Oil two 12-hole
(1-tablespoon/20ml) mini muffin pans.
2 Sift flour into medium bowl; stir in butter, eggs, corn, cheese
and chives. Divide mixture among pans.
3 Bake muffins about 15 minutes. Stand muffins in pan 5 minutes;
turn out onto wire rack to cool.

prep + cook time 30 minutes **makes** 24
nutritional count per muffin 4.1g total fat (2.5g saturated fat);
234kJ (56 cal); 8.1g carbohydrate; 1.5g protein; 0.5g fibre
storage Muffins can be stored in airtight container in refrigerator
for up to 2 days or freezer for up to 1 month.

1¼ cups (175g) gluten-free
  self-raising flour
90g butter, melted
2 eggs, beaten lightly
2 x 125g cans gluten-free
  creamed corn
½ cup (50g) pizza cheese
2 tablespoons finely chopped
  fresh chives

blueberry bubble slice

This recipe is gluten-free, wheat-free, yeast-free and egg-free.

180g white eating chocolate, melted
¾ cup (15g) puffed rice
½ cup (40g) desiccated coconut
½ cup (80g) dried blueberries
¼ cup (35g) unsalted pistachios, chopped coarsely

1 Grease 8cm x 26cm bar cake pan; line base and two long sides with baking paper, extending paper 5cm above sides.
2 Combine all ingredients in medium bowl.
3 Spoon mixture evenly into pan; refrigerate until set. Remove bubble slice from pan; cut into slices.

prep + cook time 15 minutes (+ refrigeration) **makes** 16
nutritional count per slice 6.5g total fat (3.9g saturated fat); 405kJ (97 cal); 7.9g carbohydrate; 1.5g protein; 0.7g fibre
tips You can substitute the dried blueberries for dried cranberries. Use a serrated knife for cutting the slice.
storage Slice can be stored in airtight container in the refrigerator for up to 1 week.

chocolate + fruit crackles

This recipe is gluten-free, wheat-free, yeast-free, dairy-free and egg-free.

. . . .

1 Line two 12-hole (2-tablespoons/40ml) flat-based patty pans with paper cases.
2 Combine cornflakes, rice, sultanas, meal and seeds in large bowl; stir in chocolate.
3 Spoon mixture among paper cases; press down gently, sprinkle with hundreds and thousands. Refrigerate 1 hour or until set.
prep + cook time 20 minutes (+ refrigeration) **makes** 24
nutritional count per crackle 4.4g total fat (1.9g saturated fat); 414kJ (99 cal); 12.6g carbohydrate; 1.7g protein; 0.8g fibre
storage Crackles can be stored in an airtight container in the refrigerator for up to 1 week.

2 cups (80g) gluten-free cornflakes
1 cup (20g) puffed rice
½ cup (80g) sultanas
⅓ cup (35g) hazelnut meal
2 tablespoons sunflower seeds
250g milk eating chocolate, melted
2 teaspoons gluten-free hundreds and thousands

moist flourless choc-nut cake

This recipe is gluten-free, wheat-free and yeast-free.

½ cup (50g) cocoa powder

½ cup (125ml) hot water

1½ cups (330g) firmly packed brown sugar

220g unsalted butter, chopped coarsely

200g dark eating chocolate, chopped coarsely

1½ cups (150g) hazelnut meal

6 eggs, beaten lightly

250g strawberries, sliced thinly

chocolate ganache

¾ cup (180ml) cream

300g dark eating chocolate, chopped coarsely

1 Preheat oven to 170°C/150°C fan-forced. Grease 25cm-round springform tin; line base and side with baking paper.

2 Blend cocoa with the water in medium saucepan until smooth. Add sugar, butter and chocolate; stir over low heat until smooth. Remove from heat.

3 Stand chocolate mixture about 15 minutes or until barely warm. Stir in meal and egg. Pour mixture into tin.

4 Bake cake about 1 hour 40 minutes. Cool cake in tin. Refrigerate, covered, 3 hours or overnight.

5 Meanwhile, make chocolate ganache.

6 Place cake onto serving plate. Cover with ganache, decorate with strawberries.

chocolate ganache Bring cream to the boil in small saucepan. Remove from heat, add chocolate; stir until smooth. Stand 20 minutes before using.

prep + cook time 2 hours (+ cooling and refrigeration) **serves** 16
nutritional count per serving 33.2g total fat (17.1g saturated fat); 2061kJ (493 cal); 41.6g carbohydrate; 6.7g protein; 1.8g fibre

tip This cake is a moist, dense, rich cake. Serve cut into slim wedges.

storage Undecorated cake can be stored in an airtight container in the refrigerator for up to 1 week, or freezer for up to 2 months.

carrot cupcakes

This recipe is gluten-free, wheat-free, yeast-free and nut-free.

. . . .

1 Preheat oven to 180°C/160°C fan-forced. Line 12-hole (⅓-cup/80ml) muffin pan with paper cases.

2 Beat sugar, oil and eggs in small bowl with electric mixer until thick and creamy. Transfer mixture to large bowl; stir in carrot, then sifted dry ingredients. Divide mixture among paper cases.

3 Bake cupcakes about 20 minutes. Stand cupcakes in pan 5 minutes; turn, top-side up, onto wire rack to cool.

4 Increase oven temperature to 200°C/180°C fan-forced. Grease oven trays; line with baking paper. Place lollies on trays, in batches of six to eight, about 5cm apart; bake 4 minutes. Stand on trays 2 to 3 minutes. When cool enough to handle, carefully lift shapes from trays and mould into petal shapes.

5 Make cream cheese frosting.

6 Spread cold cakes with three-quarters of the frosting. Position petals on cakes to make flowers. Drop remaining frosting into piping bag fitted with a fluted tube, pipe frosting into centre of each flower; sprinkle centres with sugar crystals.

cream cheese frosting Beat cream cheese and butter in small bowl with electric mixer until light and fluffy; gradually beat in sifted sugar.

prep + cook time 1 hour (+ cooling) **makes** 12

nutritional count per cupcake 17.5g total fat (6g saturated fat); 1455kJ (348 cal); 44.9g carbohydrate; 2.5g protein; 0.8g fibre

tip You will need about 3 medium carrots (360g) for this recipe.

storage Unfrosted cupcakes can be stored in an airtight container for up to 3 days, or freezer for up to 2 months.

⅔ cup (150g) firmly packed
   brown sugar
½ cup (125ml) vegetable oil
2 eggs
1½ cups (240g) firmly packed
   coarsely grated carrot
½ cup (75g) potato flour
¼ cup (40g) (corn) cornflour
¼ cup (50g) rice flour
1 teaspoon gluten-free
   baking powder
¼ teaspoon bicarbonate of soda
1 teaspoon mixed spice
2 x 90g packets coloured
   gluten-free sugar-free
   boiled lollies
yellow, pink and orange
   sugar crystals
cream cheese frosting
125g cream cheese, softened
50g butter, softened
½ cup (80g) pure icing sugar

passionfruit + white chocolate jelly cake

This recipe is gluten-free, wheat-free and yeast-free. You can use any flavoured jelly you like.

1 Oil deep 19cm-square cake pan with hazelnut oil. Make jelly according to packet directions; pour into pan. Refrigerate 3 hours or until set.

2 Make white chocolate ganache.

3 Pour three-quarters of ganache over the jelly; refrigerate 1 hour.

4 Meanwhile, preheat oven to 180°C/160°C fan-forced. Grease 23cm-square cake pan; line base with baking paper.

5 Beat eggs in small bowl with electric mixer until thick and creamy. Gradually beat in sugar, beating until sugar dissolves. Fold in triple-sifted cornflour. Spread mixture into pan.

6 Bake cake about 20 minutes. Turn cake onto baking-paper-covered wire rack to cool.

7 Trim cake to 19cm-square; place in pan on top of ganache and jelly. Refrigerate 30 minutes.

8 Meanwhile, spread chocolate onto baking-paper-lined tray until 3mm thick; refrigerate about 10 minutes or until set. Break into small pieces.

9 Place base of pan in sink of hot water for a few seconds to loosen jelly; quickly invert cake onto serving plate. Secure chocolate pieces around edges of cake with remaining ganache; secure ribbon.

white chocolate ganache Stir chocolate and cream in medium heatproof bowl over medium saucepan of simmering water until smooth. Cool.

prep + cook time 40 minutes (+ refrigeration) **serves** 16
nutritional count per serving 20g total fat (12.4g saturated fat); 1413kJ (338 cal); 35.4g carbohydrate; 4.3g protein; 0g fibre
storage Cake can be stored, covered, in the refrigerator for up to 2 days.

1 teaspoon hazelnut oil
85g packet passionfruit
    jelly crystals
3 eggs
½ cup (110g) caster sugar
¾ cup (110g) (corn) cornflour
150g white Choc Melts, melted
1m ribbon
white chocolate ganache
360g white eating chocolate,
    chopped coarsely
300ml cream

buttercake

This recipe is gluten-free, wheat-free and yeast-free.

. . . .

1 Preheat oven to 180°C/160°C fan-forced. Grease and line deep 25cm-heart cake pan.

2 Beat butter in medium bowl with electric mixer until changed to a paler colour. Sift flour and ¼ cup of the sugar together. Beat flour mixture and milk into the butter, in two batches only until combined.

3 Beat eggs and egg whites in small bowl with electric mixer until thick and creamy. Gradually add remaining sugar, one tablespoon at a time, beating until sugar dissolves between additions. Gradually pour egg mixture into flour mixture with motor operating on a low speed, only until combined.

4 Spread mixture into pan; bake about 50 minutes. Stand cake 10 minutes; turn, top-side up, onto wire rack to cool.

5 Make fluffy frosting. Spread top and sides of cake with pink fluffy frosting; decorate cake with roses. Spoon green fluffy frosting into small piping bag; pipe leaves onto cake.

fluffy frosting Stir sugar and the water in small saucepan over heat, without boiling, until sugar is dissolved. Boil, uncovered, without stirring about 5 minutes, or until syrup reaches 116°C on a candy thermometer. Syrup should be thick but not coloured. Remove from heat; allow bubbles to subside. Beat egg whites in small bowl with electric mixer until soft peaks form. While mixer is operating, add hot syrup in thin stream; beat on high speed about 10 minutes or until mixture is thick and cool. Reserve 2 tablespoons of the frosting in small bowl; tint green. Tint remaining icing pink.

prep + cook time 1 hour 15 minutes **serves** 12

nutritional count per serving 15.1g total fat (9.5g saturated fat); 1359kJ (325 cal); 61.4g carbohydrate; 3.1g protein; 0.4g fibre

tip For a dairy-free version of this cake, substitute dairy-free spread for the butter and soy milk for the milk.

storage Cake can be stored in an airtight container for up to 2 days. Undecorated cake can be frozen for up to 3 months.

200g butter, softened
2¼ cups (300g) gluten-free
    self-raising flour
1 cup (220g) caster sugar
½ cup (125ml) milk
2 eggs
2 egg whites
3 x 10g packets gluten-free
    edible sugar roses
fluffy frosting
1 cup (220g) caster sugar
½ cup (125ml) water
2 egg whites
green and pink food colouring

baking

Cakes, biscuits and pastries all seem to be out of reach
if you're gluten-intolerant. The 28 sensational recipes in
this chapter will delightfully prove how mistaken you are.

mandarin, macadamia + polenta cakes

This recipe is gluten-free, wheat-free and yeast-free.

1 Place whole mandarins in medium saucepan, cover with cold water; bring to the boil. Drain then repeat process twice. Cool mandarins to room temperature.

2 Preheat oven to 180°C/160°C fan-forced. Line three 6-hole (⅓-cup/80ml) muffin pans with paper cases.

3 Blend or process nuts until finely chopped; place in small bowl. Halve mandarins; discard seeds. Blend or process mandarins until pulpy.

4 Beat butter and sugar in small bowl with electric mixer until light and fluffy. Beat in eggs, one at a time. Transfer mixture to large bowl; stir in polenta, baking powder, nuts and mandarin pulp. Divide mixture among paper cases.

5 Bake cakes about 35 minutes. Stand 5 minutes before turning, top-side up, onto wire rack to cool.

6 Meanwhile, make mandarin icing.

7 Spread cold cakes with mandarin icing. Decorate with flowers.

mandarin icing Sift icing sugar into small bowl, stir in juice and butter.

prep + cook time 1 hour 15 minutes (+ cooling) **makes** 18
nutritional count per cake 25.3g total fat (10g saturated fat); 1584kJ (379 cal); 34.4g carbohydrate; 3.3g protein; 1.5g fibre
storage Cakes can be stored in an airtight container for up to 3 days.

4 small mandarins (400g)
2 cups (280g) unroasted unsalted macadamias
250g butter, softened
1 cup (220g) caster sugar
3 eggs
1 cup (170g) polenta
1 teaspoon gluten-free baking powder
gluten-free edible sugar flowers
mandarin icing
1½ cups (240g) pure icing sugar
2 tablespoons mandarin juice
20g softened butter

orange + ginger florentines

This recipe is gluten-free, wheat-free, yeast-free and egg-free.

. . . .

2 medium oranges (480g)
½ cup (110g) caster sugar
½ cup (125ml) water
2 tablespoons finely chopped
    glacé ginger
2 cups (110g) gluten-free
    rice flakes
¾ cup (60g) flaked almonds
⅔ cup (160ml) sweetened
    condensed milk
100g dark eating chocolate
    (70% cocoa solids), melted

1 Using vegetable peeler, peel orange rind from oranges; slice rind thinly. Cook rind in small saucepan of boiling water for 2 minutes; drain.
2 Return rind to small saucepan with sugar and the water; stir over heat until sugar dissolves. Bring to the boil. Boil, uncovered, 5 minutes; remove rind from pan to wire rack, discard syrup.
3 Preheat oven to 200°C/180°C fan-forced. Grease oven trays; line with baking paper.
4 Combine rind, ginger, rice flakes, nuts and milk in medium bowl. Drop level tablespoons of mixture onto trays, allowing 5cm between each florentine.
5 Bake florentines about 6 minutes or until browned lightly. Cool on trays.
6 Spread the bases of the florentines with chocolate; run fork through chocolate to make waves. Set at room temperature.
prep + cook time 40 minutes (+ standing) **makes** 22
nutritional count per florentine 3.8g total fat (1.5g saturated fat); 401kJ (96 cal); 13.3g carbohydrate; 2g protein; 0.5g fibre
storage Florentines can be stored in an airtight container for up to 2 weeks.

apple + pear crumble

This recipe is gluten-free, wheat-free, yeast-free and egg-free.

1 Preheat oven to 180°C/160°C fan-forced. Grease deep 1.5-litre (6-cup) ovenproof dish.

2 Peel, core and quarter apples and pears; slice fruit thickly. Combine fruit, sugar and the water in large saucepan; cook, covered, about 10 minutes or until fruit is just tender. Drain; discard liquid.

3 Meanwhile, make crumble topping.

4 Place apple mixture in dish; sprinkle with topping. Bake crumble about 25 minutes.

crumble topping Blend or process ingredients until combined.

prep + cook time 45 minutes **serves** 4

nutritional count per serving 21g total fat (8.7g saturated fat); 2182kJ (522 cal); 75.2g carbohydrate; 4.8g protein; 5.8g fibre

variations

muesli crumble Prepare half the amount of basic crumble mixture; stir in 1 cup (100g) toasted muesli (see page 15).

coconut crumble Prepare half the amount of basic crumble mixture; stir in ½ cup (40g) shredded coconut.

3 medium apples (450g)
3 medium pears (690g)
¼ cup (55g) caster sugar
¼ cup (60ml) water
crumble topping
½ cup (60g) almond meal
⅓ cup (65g) rice flour
⅓ cup (75g) firmly packed
   brown sugar
60g butter, chopped
1 teaspoon ground cinnamon

choc pecan cookies

This recipe is gluten-free, wheat-free and yeast-free.

. . . .

1½ cups (180g) pecan pieces
125g butter, softened
½ cup (110g) caster sugar
½ teaspoon vanilla extract
1 egg
⅔ cup (95g) brown rice flour
½ cup (75g) (corn) cornflour
150g dark eating chocolate,
　　chopped coarsely
24 whole pecans
50g dark eating chocolate,
　　melted

1 Preheat oven to 180°C/160°C fan-forced. Grease oven trays; line with baking paper.
2 Process pecan pieces until ground finely.
3 Beat butter, sugar, extract and pecan meal in small bowl with electric mixer until light and fluffy. Add egg; beat until combined. Stir in sifted flours, then chopped chocolate.
4 Roll rounded tablespoons of mixture into balls; place 7cm apart on trays, flatten slightly. Top with whole pecans.
5 Bake cookies about 20 minutes. Cool on trays.
6 Drizzle cookies with melted chocolate.
prep + cook time 55 minutes (+ cooling) **makes** 24
nutritional count per cookie 12.8g total fat (4.7g saturated fat); 777kJ (186 cal); 15.8g carbohydrate; 1.8g protein; 0.8g fibre
storage Cookies can be stored in an airtight container for up to 1 week.

raspberry cheesecake slice

This recipe is gluten-free, wheat-free and yeast-free. To ensure recipe is also nut-free, check the label on the coconut packets to ensure they do not contain traces of nuts.

1 Preheat oven to 180°C/160°C fan-forced. Grease deep 19cm-square cake pan; line base and sides with baking paper, extending paper 5cm above edges.

2 Beat egg whites lightly in medium bowl, stir in coconuts and sugar; press mixture firmly over base of pan.

3 Bake base about 15 minutes or until browned lightly. Cool.

4 Meanwhile, sprinkle gelatine over the water in small heatproof jug; stand jug in small saucepan of simmering water. Stir until gelatine dissolves. Cool 5 minutes.

5 Beat cheese and extra sugar in medium bowl with electric mixer until smooth; beat in cream and extract. Stir in gelatine mixture.

6 Sprinkle half the raspberries over base; spread with filling. Blend or process remaining raspberries; strain. Drizzle raspberry puree over cheesecake, pull skewer backwards and forwards several times for marbled effect. Refrigerate 3 hours or overnight.

prep + cook time 35 minutes (+ refrigeration) **serves** 12
nutritional count per serving 31.2g total fat (21.7g saturated fat); 1605kJ (384 cal); 19.4g carbohydrate; 6g protein; 2.8g fibre
storage Slice can be stored, covered, in the refrigerator.

2 egg whites
¾ cup (60g) desiccated coconut
¾ cup (60g) shredded coconut
⅓ cup (75g) caster sugar
3 teaspoons gelatine
¼ cup (60ml) water
500g cream cheese, softened
½ cup (110g) caster sugar, extra
300ml cream
1 teaspoon vanilla extract
300g raspberries

berry frangipane tarts

This recipe is gluten-free, wheat-free and yeast-free.

75g butter, softened
½ teaspoon vanilla extract
⅓ cup (75g) caster sugar
1 egg
¾ cup (90g) almond meal
1 tablespoon (corn) cornflour
150g fresh blueberries and
   raspberries
1 tablespoon pure icing sugar

1 Preheat oven to 180°C/160°C fan-forced. Grease six 5.5cm x 10.5cm loose-based fluted flan tins; place on oven tray.

2 Beat butter, extract and caster sugar in small bowl with electric mixer until light and fluffy. Add egg; beat until combined. Stir in meal and cornflour. Spoon mixture into tins; smooth surface, sprinkle with berries.

3 Bake tarts about 30 minutes. Stand in tins 10 minutes; turn carefully, top-side up, onto baking-paper-covered wire rack.

4 Serve tarts warm or cold, dusted with sifted icing sugar.

prep + cook time 45 minutes **makes** 6
nutritional count per tart 19.5g total fat (7.6g saturated fat); 1133kJ (271 cal); 18.8g carbohydrate; 4.4g protein; 2.2g fibre
storage Tarts can be stored in an airtight container for up to 2 days.

passionfruit kisses

This recipe is gluten-free, wheat-free, yeast-free and dairy-free.

- -

1 Preheat oven to 180°C/160°C fan-forced. Grease four 12-hole (1½-tablespoons/30ml) round-based patty pans.
2 Beat eggs in small bowl with electric mixer until thick and creamy. Add sugar, one tablespoon at a time, beating until sugar dissolves between additions. Gently fold in triple-sifted cornflour. Drop one level tablespoon of mixture into each pan hole.
3 Bake cakes about 10 minutes. Turn cakes immediately onto baking-paper-covered wire rack by tapping upside-down pans firmly on the bench to release the cakes; cool.
4 Meanwhile, make passionfruit filling.
5 Sandwich cold kisses with passionfruit filling; serve dusted with sifted icing sugar.

passionfruit filling Beat spread in small bowl with electric mixer until as white as possible; gradually beat in sifted icing sugar. Stir in passionfruit.

prep + cook time 40 minutes (+ cooling) **makes** 24
nutritional count per kiss 3.7g total fat (0.7g saturated fat); 485kJ (116 cal); 19.5g carbohydrate; 0.9g protein; 0.3g fibre
storage Kisses can be stored in an airtight container for 1 day. Unfilled kisses can be frozen for up to 3 months.

3 eggs
½ cup (110g) caster sugar
¾ cup (110g) (corn) cornflour
2 tablespoons pure icing sugar
passionfruit filling
90g dairy-free spread
1½ cups (240g) pure icing sugar
2 tablespoons passionfruit pulp

chocolate fudge brownies

This recipe is gluten-free, wheat-free and yeast-free.

150g butter, chopped coarsely

300g dark eating chocolate, chopped coarsely

1½ cups (330g) firmly packed brown sugar

3 eggs

¾ cup (75g) hazelnut meal

½ cup (75g) buckwheat flour

½ cup (120g) sour cream

¼ cup (25g) cocoa powder

1 Preheat oven to 180°C/160°C fan-forced. Grease 19cm x 29cm slice pan; line base with baking paper, extending paper 5cm over two long sides.

2 Melt butter and chocolate in medium saucepan over low heat. Stir in sugar; cook, stirring, 2 minutes. Cool 10 minutes.

3 Stir in eggs, then meal, flour, sour cream and 2 tablespoons of the sifted cocoa. Spread mixture into pan.

4 Bake brownies about 45 minutes. Cool in pan before cutting into squares. Serve dusted with remaining sifted cocoa.

prep + cook time 1 hour 10 minutes (+ cooling) **makes** 18

nutritional count per brownie 18g total fat (9.6g saturated fat); 1275kJ (305 cal); 32g carbohydrate; 3.6g protein; 0.8g fibre

storage Brownies can be stored in an airtight container in the refrigerator for up to 4 days.

chocolate apple cake

This recipe is gluten-free, wheat-free, yeast-free and dairy-free.

1 Preheat oven to 180°C/160°C fan-forced. Grease 20cm x 30cm lamington pan; line base with baking paper, extending paper 5cm over two long sides.

2 Peel apples; grate coarsely. Chop grated apple finely.

3 Sift dry ingredients into large bowl; stir in apple, meal, eggs, oil and extract. Pour mixture into pan.

4 Bake cake about 45 minutes. Turn, top-side up, onto wire rack to cool.

5 Meanwhile, make chocolate icing.

6 Spread cold cake with chocolate icing.

chocolate icing Sift sugar and cocoa into small bowl; stir in enough juice to make a thick icing.

prep + cook time 1 hour 10 minutes (+ cooling) **serves** 18

nutritional count per serving 15g total fat (2.2g saturated fat); 1191kJ (285 cal); 34.7g carbohydrate; 2.6g protein; 1.3g fibre

tip Use a hot dry knife to cut the cake.

storage Cake can be stored in an airtight container for up to 3 days. Un-iced cake is suitable to freeze for up to 3 months.

4 medium apples (600g)
¾ cup (110g) potato flour
¾ cup (100g) brown rice flour
¼ cup (25g) cocoa powder
1 cup (220g) caster sugar
1 teaspoon bicarbonate of soda
¼ cup (30g) linseed meal
4 eggs, beaten lightly
1 cup (250ml) vegetable oil
1 teaspoon vanilla extract

chocolate icing

1 cup (160g) pure icing sugar
1 tablespoon cocoa powder
2 tablespoons apple juice, approximately

kumara dampers

This recipe is gluten-free, wheat-free, yeast-free and egg-free.

1⅔ cups (225g) gluten-free
   self-raising flour
1 teaspoon caster sugar
¼ teaspoon salt
20g butter
½ cup cold mashed sieved
   cooked kumara
½ cup (125ml) buttermilk
2 tablespoons water,
   approximately
2 teaspoons milk, approximately
2 teaspoons gluten-free
   self-raising flour, extra

1 Preheat oven to 220°C/200°C fan-forced. Oil oven tray.
2 Sift dry ingredients into large bowl; rub in the butter. Add kumara, buttermilk and enough of the water to mix to a soft, sticky dough. Knead dough lightly on floured surface until smooth.
3 Divide dough into four equal portions. Roll each portion into rounds, place on tray. Cut cross through top of dough, about 5mm deep. Brush tops with milk, then dust with extra sifted flour.
4 Bake dampers about 35 minutes.

prep + cook time 50 minutes **makes** 4
nutritional count per damper 5.2g total fat (3.2g saturated fat); 543kJ (130 cal); 56.5g carbohydrate; 2.8g protein; 1.5g fibre
tip You will need to cook 250g kumara for this recipe.
storage Dampers are best made and eaten on the same day. They can be frozen for up to 3 months. Thaw in the oven, wrapped in foil.

lime curd meringue tarts

This recipe is gluten-free, wheat-free, yeast-free and dairy-free.

1 Preheat oven to 130°C/110°C fan-forced. Line 6-hole (⅓-cup/80ml) muffin pan with paper cases.

2 Beat egg whites in small bowl with electric mixer until soft peaks form; gradually add sugars, one tablespoon at a time, beating until sugar dissolves between additions.

3 Spoon meringue into paper cases; using the back of a metal spoon, make a small hollow in each meringue.

4 Bake meringues about 1 hour; cool in oven with door ajar.

5 Meanwhile, make lime curd.

6 Serve meringues topped with curd, then mint leaves. Dust with extra sifted icing sugar.

lime curd Strain eggs into medium heatproof bowl, stir in sugar, spread and juice; stir over medium saucepan of simmering water until mixture thickens and coats the back of a wooden spoon. Remove from heat. Stand bowl in sink of cold water, stirring occasionally, about 10 minutes or until cold. Stir in rind and tint with food colouring. Cover; refrigerate 1 hour or until thick.

prep + cook time 1 hour 15 minutes (+ refrigeration) **makes** 6
nutritional count per meringue 13.9g total fat (2.7g saturated fat); 1225kJ (293 cal); 38.4g carbohydrate; 3.6g protein; 0.9g fibre
tip You will need about 3 limes for this recipe.
storage Meringues are best made and eaten on the same day. Top meringues with curd just before serving.

2 egg whites
½ cup (110g) caster sugar
2 teaspoons pure icing sugar
6 fresh mint leaves
1 teaspoon pure icing sugar, extra

lime curd

2 eggs, beaten lightly
½ cup (110g) caster sugar
90g dairy-free spread
⅓ cup (80ml) lime juice
2 teaspoons finely grated lime rind
green food colouring

chocolate strawberry tart

This recipe is gluten-free, wheat-free and yeast-free.

⅓ cup (110g) strawberry jam

⅔ cup (160ml) cream

25g unsalted butter

200g dark eating chocolate, chopped finely

6 strawberries, halved

hazelnut crust

1½ cups (150g) hazelnut meal

⅓ cup (75g) caster sugar

¼ cup (35g) (corn) cornflour

125g cold unsalted butter, chopped

1 egg yolk

1 Make hazelnut crust.

2 Grease 22cm-round loose-based flan tin. Roll hazelnut dough between sheets of baking paper until large enough to line tin. Ease dough into tin, press into base and side; trim edge. Cover; refrigerate 30 minutes.

3 Preheat oven to 200°C/180°C fan-forced.

4 Place tin on oven tray. Bake hazelnut crust about 25 minutes. Spread jam over crust; return to oven 2 minutes. Cool.

5 Heat cream in medium saucepan; remove from heat, stir in butter and chocolate, then whisk until smooth. Pour chocolate mixture into crust; refrigerate 2 hours. Top tart with strawberries.

hazelnut crust Process meal, sugar, cornflour and butter until crumbly; add egg yolk, pulse until mixture comes together. Knead dough gently on floured surface until smooth. Wrap in plastic; refrigerate 1 hour.

prep + cook time 50 minutes (+ refrigeration) **serves** 12

nutritional count per serving 29.1g total fat (14g saturated fat); 1597kJ (382 cal); 26.6g carbohydrate; 3.4g protein; 1.8g fibre

storage Tart can be stored in an airtight container in the refrigerator, for up to 2 days.

coconut custard tarts

This recipe is gluten-free, wheat-free and yeast-free.

1 Preheat oven to 180°C/160°C fan-forced. Grease 12-hole (⅓-cup/80ml) muffin pan.

2 Combine coconuts and sugar in large bowl; stir in egg whites. Press mixture over base and side of pan holes to make cases.

3 Whisk egg yolks, extra sugar and arrowroot together in medium saucepan; gradually whisk in milk and cream to make custard.

4 Split vanilla bean in half lengthways; scrape seeds into custard, discard pod. Add lemon rind to custard; stir over medium heat until mixture boils and thickens slightly. Remove from heat immediately; discard rind.

5 Spoon warm custard into pastry cases; bake about 15 minutes or until set and browned lightly. Stand tarts in pan for 10 minutes. Transfer to wire rack to cool.

6 Serve tarts dusted with sifted icing sugar.

prep + cook time 45 minutes (+ standing and cooling) **makes** 12
nutritional count per tart 19.3g total fat (15.1g saturated fat); 1233kJ (295 cal); 25.4g carbohydrate; 3.9g protein; 2.9g fibre
storage Tarts can be stored in an airtight container in the refrigerator for up to 2 days.

1½ cups (120g) desiccated coconut
1½ cups (115g) shredded coconut
⅔ cup (150g) caster sugar
4 egg whites, beaten lightly
3 egg yolks
½ cup (110g) caster sugar, extra
1 tablespoon arrowroot
¾ cup (180ml) milk
½ cup (125ml) cream
1 vanilla bean
5cm strip lemon rind
1 tablespoon pure icing sugar

self-saucing jaffa pudding

This recipe is gluten-free, wheat-free, yeast-free, egg-free and nut-free.

60g butter

½ cup (125ml) milk

½ teaspoon vanilla extract

¾ cup (165g) caster sugar

½ cup (100g) rice flour

⅓ cup (40g) soya flour

⅓ cup (45g) gluten-free
  self-raising flour

1 teaspoon gluten-free
  baking powder

2 tablespoons cocoa powder

2 teaspoons finely grated
  orange rind

½ cup (110g) firmly packed
  brown sugar

2 cups (500ml) boiling water

1 Preheat oven to 180°C/160°C fan-forced. Grease 1.5-litre (6-cup) ovenproof dish.

2 Melt butter with milk and extract in medium saucepan. Remove from heat; whisk in caster sugar, then sifted flours, baking powder, half the cocoa and rind. Spread mixture into dish.

3 Sift brown sugar and the remaining cocoa over mixture; gently pour the boiling water over mixture.

4 Bake pudding about 40 minutes. Stand 5 minutes before serving.

prep + cook time 1 hour **serves** 6

nutritional count per serving 11g total fat (6.4g saturated fat); 1568kJ (375 cal); 68.1g carbohydrate; 4.8g protein; 1.3g fibre

storage Pudding can be stored in an airtight container in the refrigerator for up to 2 days.

lime + coconut friands

This recipe is gluten-free, wheat-free, yeast-free and nut-free.

1 Preheat oven 200°C/180°C fan-forced. Grease 12-hole (½-cup/125ml) friand pan.

2 Whisk egg whites in large bowl with fork until combined. Add butter, meal, desiccated coconut, sifted sugar and flour, rind and juice; stir until combined. Divide mixture among pan holes.

3 Bake friands for 10 minutes. Remove pan from oven, sprinkle with flaked coconut; bake further 10 minutes. Stand in pan 5 minutes; turn, top-side up, onto wire rack to cool.

prep + cook time 30 minutes (+ cooling) **makes** 12

nutritional count per friand 18.6g total fat (11.1g saturated fat); 1170kJ (280 cal); 23.6g carbohydrate; 4.8g protein; 3g fibre

tip If the coconut is browning too quickly, cover the friands loosely with foil.

storage Friands can be stored in an airtight container for up to 3 days.

6 egg whites
185g butter, melted
¾ cup (90g) linseed meal
½ cup (40g) desiccated coconut
1½ cups (240g) pure icing sugar
⅓ cup (40g) soya flour
2 teaspoons finely grated lime rind
2 tablespoons lime juice
¼ cup (10g) flaked coconut

coconut rice puddings

This recipe is gluten-free, wheat-free, yeast-free and dairy-free.

4 eggs
⅓ cup (75g) caster sugar
1 teaspoon vanilla extract
400ml can coconut cream
1½ cups (375ml) gluten-free
   soy milk
1 cup cooked white
   medium-grain rice
½ cup (80g) sultanas
½ teaspoon ground cinnamon

1 Preheat oven to 180°C/160°C fan-forced. Grease six ¾-cup (180ml) ovenproof dishes.

2 Whisk eggs, sugar and extract in large jug until combined; whisk in cream and soy milk. Stir in rice and sultanas. Divide mixture evenly among dishes; place dishes in large baking dish. Add enough boiling water to come halfway up sides of small dishes.

3 Bake puddings 20 minutes, whisking gently with fork under the skin of the puddings twice – this stops the rice sinking to the bottom of the dishes. Sprinkle puddings with cinnamon; bake further 20 minutes or until set. Stand puddings 10 minutes before serving.

prep + cook time 1 hour **makes** 6

nutritional count per pudding 19.7g total fat (13.4g saturated fat); 1530kJ (366 cal); 37.2g carbohydrate; 9.1g protein; 2.3g fibre

tip You will need to cook ⅓ cup (65g) white medium-grain rice for this recipe.

storage Puddings can be stored, covered, in the refrigerator for up to 2 days.

lemon tarts

This recipe is gluten-free, wheat-free, yeast-free and nut-free.

1 Process flours, caster sugar and butter until crumbly; add enough of the water to make ingredients come together. Knead dough gently on floured surface until smooth.

2 Preheat oven to 180°C/160°C fan-forced. Grease six 10cm deep loose-based flan tins.

3 Divide pastry into six portions. Roll one portion at a time between sheets of baking paper until large enough to line tins. Ease pastry into tins, pressing into base and side; trim edges, prick base with fork. Cover; refrigerate 30 minutes.

4 Place tins on oven tray; cover pastry with baking paper, fill with dried beans or uncooked rice. Bake 10 minutes; remove paper and beans carefully from pastry cases. Bake further 10 minutes; cool.

5 Reduce oven temperature to 160°C/140°C fan-forced.

6 Make lemon filling; divide filling among pastry cases.

7 Bake tarts about 30 minutes or until the surface is firm to touch. Remove from oven; cool. Refrigerate 2 hours before serving dusted with sifted icing sugar.

lemon filling Whisk mascarpone and eggs together in large jug until smooth. Add sifted sugar, rind and juice; whisk until smooth.

prep + cook time 1 hour 15 minutes (+ standing and refrigeration)

makes 6

nutritional count per tart 45.4g total fat (28.4g saturated fat); 3043kJ (728 cal); 68.6g carbohydrate; 11g protein; 1.5g fibre

storage Tarts can be stored in an airtight container in the refrigerator for up to 2 days.

1¼ cups (250g) rice flour
¼ cup (35g) (corn) cornflour
¼ cup (30g) soya flour
⅓ cup (75g) caster sugar
150g cold butter,
    chopped coarsely
¼ cup (60ml) cold water,
    approximately
1 tablespoon pure icing sugar
lemon filling
1 cup (250g) mascarpone cheese
4 eggs
½ cup (80g) pure icing sugar
1 tablespoon finely grated
    lemon rind
½ cup (125ml) lemon juice

banana bread

This recipe is gluten-free, wheat-free, yeast-free, dairy-free and egg-free.

2 tablespoons desiccated
  coconut
1½ cups mashed overripe
  banana
1¼ cups (275g) firmly packed
  brown sugar
½ cup (125ml) vegetable oil
2 teaspoons gluten-free
  baking powder
1 teaspoon mixed spice
2½ cups (200g) desiccated
  coconut, extra
1¾ cups (225g) linseed,
  sunflower and almond meal

1 Preheat oven to 180°C/160°C fan-forced. Grease 11cm x 21cm loaf pan; coat base and sides with desiccated coconut. Shake out excess coconut.

2 Combine banana, sugar, oil, baking powder and spice in large bowl, stir in extra coconut and meal. Spread mixture into pan; smooth surface.

3 Bake bread about 55 minutes. Stand in pan 10 minutes; turn, top-side up, onto baking-paper-covered wire rack to cool.

prep + cook time 1 hour 10 minutes (+ cooling) **makes** 10 slices
nutritional count per slice 34.3g total fat (16.2g saturated fat); 2119kJ (507 cal); 41.4g carbohydrate; 7.4g protein; 5g fibre
tips You will need 3 large overripe bananas (690g) for this recipe. This banana bread is good sliced and toasted.

storage Banana bread can be stored in an airtight container in the refrigerator for up to 1 week.

passionfruit + lime crème brûlée

This recipe is gluten-free, wheat-free, yeast-free, dairy-free and nut-free.

1 Preheat oven to 180°C/160°C fan-forced.

2 Combine passionfruit, egg, egg yolks, caster sugar and rind in medium heatproof bowl.

3 Bring coconut cream and milk to the boil in small saucepan. Gradually whisk hot cream mixture into egg mixture. Place bowl over medium saucepan of simmering water; stir over heat about 10 minutes or until custard thickens slightly.

4 Divide custard among four deep ½-cup (125ml) heatproof dishes. Place dishes in medium baking dish; pour enough boiling water into baking dish to come halfway up sides of dishes. Bake about 40 minutes or until custard is set. Remove custards from water; cool. Cover; refrigerate 3 hours or overnight.

5 Preheat grill.

6 Place custards in shallow flameproof dish filled with ice cubes. Sprinkle each custard with 1 teaspoon brown sugar; using finger, gently smooth sugar over the surface of each custard. Place dish under grill until sugar caramelises.

prep + cook time 1 hour (+ cooling and refrigeration) **serves** 4
nutritional count per serving 19.4g total fat (14.1g saturated fat); 1124kJ (269 cal); 16.6g carbohydrate; 5.9g protein; 3.5g fibre

¼ cup (60ml) passionfruit pulp
1 egg
2 egg yolks
2 tablespoons caster sugar
1 teaspoon finely grated lime rind
280ml can coconut cream
½ cup (125ml) gluten-free soy milk
1 tablespoon brown sugar

potato scones

This recipe is gluten-free, wheat-free, yeast-free and nut-free.

125g butter, softened
⅓ cup (55g) pure icing sugar
2 egg yolks
1 cup cold mashed sieved
  cooked potato
2 cups (270g) gluten-free
  self-raising flour
2 teaspoons gluten-free
  baking powder
2 teaspoons milk, approximately
¼ cup (80g) raspberry jam
¼ cup (60ml) double thick cream

1 Preheat oven to 220°C/200°C fan-forced. Grease oven tray.
2 Beat butter, sifted sugar and egg yolks in small bowl with electric mixer until light and fluffy. Transfer to large bowl; stir in mashed potato.
3 Stir in sifted flour and baking powder; mix to a soft dough. Knead dough lightly on floured surface until smooth.
4 Press dough out to an even 2.5cm thickness. Dip 5cm-round cutter into flour; cut as many rounds as possible from the dough. Place scones 3cm apart on tray. Gently knead scraps of dough together; repeat process.
5 Brush tops of scones with milk; bake about 25 minutes or until scones sound hollow when tapped firmly on the top. Serve with jam and cream.

prep + cook time 40 minutes **makes** 12
nutritional count per scone 11.5g total fat (7.2g saturated fat); 732kJ (175 cal); 31.5g carbohydrate; 1.6g protein; 0.8g fibre
tip You will need to cook 1 large potato (300g) for this recipe.
storage Scones are best made and eaten on the same day. They can be frozen for up to 3 months. Thaw in oven, wrapped in foil.

chocolate cupcakes

This recipe is gluten-free, wheat-free, yeast-free and dairy-free.

. . . .

1 Preheat oven to 150°C/130°C fan-forced. Line 12-hole (⅓-cup/80ml) muffin pan with paper cases.
2 Stir spread, chocolate, milk and sugar in medium saucepan over low heat until smooth. Transfer to large bowl; cool 10 minutes. Whisk in sifted flours and cocoa until smooth. Divide mixture among paper cases.
3 Bake cupcakes about 35 minutes. Stand in pan 10 minutes; turn, top-side up, onto wire rack to cool.
4 Meanwhile, make fudge frosting.
5 Using 2cm fluted tube, pipe fudge frosting onto cold cupcakes.
fudge frosting Stir caster sugar, spread and the water in small saucepan over low heat until sugar dissolves. Combine sifted icing sugar and cocoa in small bowl; gradually stir in hot sugar mixture until smooth. Cover; refrigerate 20 minutes. Beat frosting until spreadable.
prep + cook time 1 hour 10 minutes (+ cooling and refrigeration)
makes 12
nutritional count per cupcake 14.9g total fat (3.8g saturated fat); 1292kJ (309 cal); 49.4g carbohydrate; 1.6g protein; 0.6g fibre
storage Cupcakes can be stored in an airtight container in the refrigerator for up to 3 days.

125g dairy-free spread
100g dark eating chocolate (70% cocoa solids), chopped coarsely
¾ cup (180ml) gluten-free soy milk
¾ cup (165g) caster sugar
1 cup (135g) gluten-free self-raising flour
½ cup (70g) gluten-free plain flour
2 tablespoons cocoa powder
fudge frosting
¼ cup (55g) caster sugar
50g dairy-free spread
2 tablespoons water
¾ cup (120g) pure icing sugar
2 tablespoons cocoa powder

sticky date cakes with orange caramel sauce

This recipe is gluten-free, wheat-free, yeast-free and dairy-free.

1 cup (140g) seeded dried dates
¾ cup (180ml) boiling water
1 teaspoon bicarbonate of soda
125g dairy-free spread
¾ cup (165g) firmly packed
　　brown sugar
4 eggs
2 cups (240g) almond meal
½ cup (40g) desiccated coconut
½ cup (100g) rice flour

orange caramel sauce
50g dairy-free spread
½ cup (110g) firmly packed
　　brown sugar
⅓ cup (80ml) orange juice

1 Preheat oven to 180°C/160°C fan-forced. Grease two 6-hole texas (¾-cup/180ml) muffin pans; line base of each pan hole with baking paper.

2 Combine dates, the water and soda in bowl of food processor. Place lid in position; stand 5 minutes. Process until almost smooth.

3 Meanwhile, beat spread and sugar in small bowl with electric mixer until light and fluffy. Beat in eggs, one at a time (mixture will curdle). Transfer to large bowl; stir in almond meal, coconut and sifted flour, then the date mixture. Divide mixture among pan holes.

4 Bake cakes about 25 minutes. Stand in pan 5 minutes before serving.

5 Make orange caramel sauce.

6 Serve warm cakes with hot orange caramel sauce.

orange caramel sauce Melt spread in small frying pan. Add sugar; stir over heat until dissolved. Add juice; cook, stirring, until sauce thickens slightly.

prep + cook time 50 minutes　**makes** 12

nutritional count per cake 23.5g total fat (4.7g saturated fat); 1672kJ (400 cal); 38.5g carbohydrate; 7.3g protein; 3.6g fibre

tip You can substitute the almond meal for hazelnut or pecan meal if you prefer.

storage The orange caramel sauce is best served immediately once prepared because it will separate on standing.

brazil nut bread

This recipe is gluten-free, wheat-free, yeast-free and dairy-free.

. . . .

1 Preheat oven to 180°C/160°C fan-forced. Grease and line 8cm x 26cm bar cake pan.

2 Beat egg whites in small bowl with electric mixer until soft peaks form. Gradually add sugar, one tablespoon at a time, beating until sugar dissolves between additions.

3 Transfer mixture to medium bowl; fold in sifted flour and rind, then nuts. Spread into pan.

4 Bake bread about 30 minutes; cool in pan. Wrap bread in foil; refrigerate 3 hours or overnight.

5 Preheat oven to 150°C/130°C fan-forced.

6 Using serrated knife, cut bread into 3mm slices; place slices in a single layer on baking-paper-lined oven trays. Bake about 15 minutes or until crisp.

prep + cook time 1 hour (+ refrigeration and cooling) **makes** 48 slices
nutritional count per slice 2.3g total fat (0.5g saturated fat); 146kJ (35 cal); 2.9g carbohydrate; 0.7g protein; 0.3g fibre
storage Brazil nut bread can be stored in an airtight container for up to 1 week.

2 egg whites
⅓ cup (75g) caster sugar
½ cup (70g) gluten-free
  plain flour
1 teaspoon finely grated
  orange rind
1 cup (160g) brazil nuts

christmas pudding

This recipe is gluten-free, wheat-free, yeast-free, dairy-free and egg-free.

2 cups (320g) sultanas

1½ cups (225g) coarsely
  chopped raisins

1 cup (140g) coarsely chopped
  seeded dried dates

1 cup (190g) coarsely chopped
  dried figs

½ cup (70g) slivered almonds

1½ cups (375ml) water

1 cup (220g) firmly packed
  brown sugar

185g dairy-free spread

½ cup (125ml) brandy

2 tablespoons golden syrup

1 cup (125g) soya flour

1 cup (150g) rice flour

2 teaspoons mixed spice

1 teaspoon cream of tartar

½ teaspoon bicarbonate of soda

1 cup (120g) almond meal

1 Stir fruit, nuts, the water, sugar, spread, brandy and golden syrup in large saucepan over low heat until spread melts. Transfer mixture to large heatproof bowl; cool.

2 Grease 2.25-litre (9-cup) pudding steamer; line base with baking paper.

3 Stir sifted dry ingredients and almond meal into fruit mixture. Spoon mixture into steamer, cover pudding with greased foil; secure with lid or kitchen string.

4 Place steamer in large saucepan with enough boiling water to come halfway up side of steamer; simmer, covered, about 6 hours, replenishing water as necessary to maintain level. Stand in steamer 10 minutes before turning pudding out.

prep + cook time 6 hours 15 minutes **serves** 12

nutritional count per serving 23.9g total fat (3.2g saturated fat); 2621kJ (627 cal); 83.5g carbohydrate; 9.8g protein; 8.2g fibre

tips Chop all fruit a similar size to the sultanas. Use orange juice instead of brandy, if you like. Cut holly leaves from lightweight card; bend gently to shape.

storage Pudding can be stored, covered, in the refrigerator for up to 1 month.

fruit cakes

This recipe is gluten-free, wheat-free, yeast-free, dairy-free and nut-free.

. . . .

1 Line six 9cm-round cake pans with two thicknesses of baking paper, extending paper 5cm above side.

2 Stir sultanas, raisins, currants, peel, chopped pineapple, spread, sugar, brandy and the water in medium saucepan over medium heat until spread is melted and sugar is dissolved; bring to the boil. Remove from heat; transfer to large heatproof bowl. Cool.

3 Preheat oven to 150°C/130°C fan-forced.

4 Stir eggs into fruit mixture then sifted dry ingredients. Divide mixture among pans; decorate with cherries and pineapple wedges.

5 Bake cakes about 1 hour 10 minutes. Cover hot cakes with foil; cool in pans overnight.

prep + cook time 1 hour 30 minutes (+ cooling) **makes** 6
nutritional count per cake 31.4g total fat (5.9g saturated fat); 3963kJ (948 cal); 141g carbohydrate; 13.1g protein; 7g fibre

tip When buying glacé fruit check the ingredients label for signs of 'glucose made from wheat' – glacé fruit is available without glucose, making it gluten-free and wheat-free.

storage Cakes can be stored in an airtight container in the refrigerator for up to 1 month.

1½ cups (240g) sultanas
1 cup (170g) raisins, chopped coarsely
1 cup (160g) dried currants
2 tablespoons finely chopped mixed peel
⅓ cup (75g) coarsely chopped glacé pineapple
185g dairy-free spread
¾ cup (165g) firmly packed brown sugar
⅓ cup (80ml) brandy
⅓ cup (80ml) water
3 eggs
¾ cup (150g) rice flour
¾ cup (90g) soya flour
3 teaspoons gluten-free baking powder
1 teaspoon ground cinnamon
1 teaspoon ground nutmeg
½ teaspoon ground clove
18 green glacé cherries, halved
3 slices glacé pineapple, cut into wedges

orange shortbread

This recipe is gluten-free, wheat-free, yeast-free, egg-free and nut-free.

· ·

250g butter, softened

3 teaspoons finely grated
orange rind

½ cup (110g) caster sugar

1¾ cups (240g) gluten-free
plain flour

⅓ cup (65g) rice flour

1 tablespoon white sugar

1 Preheat oven to 150°C/130°C fan-forced. Grease two oven trays.

2 Beat butter, rind and caster sugar in small bowl with electric mixer until light and fluffy. Transfer mixture to large bowl; stir in sifted flours in two batches. Knead dough lightly on floured surface until smooth.

3 Divide dough in half; shape each, on separate trays, into 20cm rounds. Mark each round into twelve wedges; prink with fork. Pinch edges of rounds with fingers; sprinkle with white sugar.

4 Bake shortbread about 40 minutes. Stand 5 minutes; then, using sharp knife, cut shortbread into wedges. Cool on trays.

prep + cook time 1 hour (+ cooling) **makes** 24

nutritional count per shortbread 8.6g total fat (5.6g saturated fat); 606kJ (145 cal); 16.3g carbohydrate; 0.4g protein; 0.2g fibre

tip Try substituting the orange rind for lemon rind and add ⅓ cup (45g) coarsely chopped dried cranberries to the dough.

storage Shortbread can be stored in an airtight container for up to 1 week.

fruit mince tarts

This recipe is gluten-free, wheat-free, yeast-free, egg-free and nut-free.

. . . .

1 Make pastry.

2 Combine fruit, brandy, the water, brown sugar and spice in small saucepan; stir over low heat until sugar dissolves. Bring to the boil. Reduce heat; simmer, stirring, until liquid is absorbed and fruit is plump and tender. Stir in rind; cool. Blend or process cold fruit mixture until mixture forms a paste.

3 Preheat oven to 200°C/180°C fan-forced. Grease 12-hole (1½-tablespoons/30ml) shallow round-based patty pan.

4 Roll pastry between sheets of baking paper until 5mm thick; cut 12 x 7cm rounds from pastry. Ease pastry rounds into pan holes, press into base and side; prick bases with fork. Spoon fruit mixture into pastry cases. Cut six 5cm stars; top six tarts with stars. Cut six 6cm rounds from remaining pastry; cut 3cm stars from each round, discard these stars. Place rounds on remaining six tarts. Brush tops with a little extra water. Sprinkle tarts with caster sugar.

5 Bake tarts about 15 minutes. Serve dusted with sifted icing sugar.

pastry Process flours, sugar and butter until fine. Add enough of the water to make ingredients come together. Cover; refrigerate 30 minutes.

prep + cook time 50 minutes (+ refrigeration and cooling) **makes** 12
nutritional count per tart 11.2g total fat (6.9g saturated fat); 1287kJ (308 cal); 43g carbohydrate; 2.6g protein; 1.7g fibre
storage Tarts can be stored in an airtight container for up to 3 days. Fruit mince mixture will keep in an airtight container in the refrigerator for up to 1 month.

½ cup (80g) coarsely
  chopped raisins
½ cup (80g) sultanas
⅓ cup (45g) dried cranberries
⅓ cup (25g) finely chopped
  dried apple
½ cup (125ml) brandy
¼ cup (60ml) water
2 tablespoons brown sugar
1 teaspoon mixed spice
1 teaspoon finely grated
  lemon rind
1 teaspoon caster sugar
2 teaspoons pure icing sugar
pastry
1¼ cups (250g) rice flour
¼ cup (35g) (corn) cornflour
¼ cup (30g) soya flour
⅓ cup (75g) caster sugar
150g cold butter, chopped
2 tablespoons cold water,
  approximately

strawberry meringue cakes

This recipe is gluten-free, wheat-free and yeast-free.

200g butter, softened

2¼ cups (300g) gluten-free
self-raising flour

1 cup (220g) caster sugar

½ cup (125ml) milk

2 eggs

2 egg whites

½ cup (160g) strawberry jam

3 egg whites, extra

¾ cup (165g) caster sugar, extra

1 Preheat oven to 180°C/160°C fan-forced. Line two 12-hole (⅓-cup/80ml) muffin pans with paper cases.

2 Beat butter in medium bowl with electric mixer until changed to a lighter colour. Sift flour and ¼-cup of the caster sugar together; beat flour mixture and milk into butter, in two batches, only until combined.

3 Beat eggs and egg whites in small bowl with electric mixer until thick and creamy. Gradually add remaining sugar, one tablespoon at a time, beating until sugar dissolves between additions. Gradually beat egg mixture into flour mixture only until combined.

4 Divide mixture among paper cases; bake cakes about 20 minutes. Transfer, top-side up to wire rack to cool.

5 Increase oven temperature to 220°C/200°C fan-forced.

6 Cut deep 2cm wide hole from centre of each cake; discard cake tops. Fill holes with jam.

7 Beat extra egg whites in small bowl with electric mixer until soft peaks form. Gradually add extra sugar, one tablespoon at a time, beating until sugar dissolves between additions. Spoon meringue mixture into large piping bag fitted with 1cm plain tube. Place cakes on oven trays; pipe meringue on top of each cake. Bake 5 minutes or until meringue is browned lightly.

prep + cook time 40 minutes (+ cooling) **makes** 24

nutritional count per cake 7.6g total fat (4.8g saturated fat); 702kJ (168 cal); 31.7g carbohydrate; 1.7g protein; 0.3g fibre

tip For a dairy-free version of this cake, substitute dairy-free spread for the butter and soy milk for the milk.

storage Cakes can be stored in an airtight container for up to 2 days. Unfilled cakes can be frozen for up to 3 months.

glossary

almonds
flaked paper-thin slices.
meal almonds ground to a coarse flour texture.
slivered small pieces cut lengthways.
arrowroot a starch made from the rhizome of a
Central American plant, used mostly as a thickener.
bacon rashers also called bacon slices.
baking powder a raising agent; consists of two
parts cream of tartar to one part bicarbonate of soda.
Gluten-free baking powder is made without cereals.
bicarbonate of soda also called baking soda.
brazil nuts a triangular-shelled oily nut with an
unusually tender white flesh and a mild, rich flavour.
butter use salted or unsalted (sweet); 125g is
equal to one stick (4 ounces) butter.
buttermilk is commercially made like yogurt;
sold alongside dairy products in supermarkets.
cheese
cream commonly called Philadelphia or Philly, a
soft cow milk cheese with a fat content of at least
33%. Sold at supermarkets in bulk and packaged.
fetta Greek in origin; a crumbly goat- or sheep-
milk cheese with a sharp, salty taste.
mascarpone an Italian fresh cultured-cream product
made like yogurt. Whiteish to creamy yellow with a
buttery-rich texture. Soft, creamy and spreadable.
parmesan a hard, grainy cow-milk cheese.
pizza a commercial blend of varying proportions
of grated mozzarella, cheddar and parmesan.
ricotta a sweet, moist, soft, white, cows-milk
cheese; has a slightly grainy texture.
chicken tenderloins thin strip under the breast.
chocolate
Choc Melts small discs of compounded milk, white
or dark chocolate, ideal for melting and moulding.

dark eating (70% cocoa solids) also called semi-
sweet; made of a high percentage of cocoa liquor
and cocoa butter, and little added sugar. We use
dark eating chocolate unless stated otherwise.
white eating contains no cocoa solids, deriving its
sweetness from cocoa butter. Very sensitive to heat.
cinnamon dried inner bark of the shoots of the
cinnamon tree; comes in sticks (quills) and ground.
cloves dried flower buds of a tropical tree; can be
used whole or ground. They have a strong scent
and taste so should be used sparingly.
cocoa powder also called unsweetened cocoa.
coconut
cream obtained commercially from the first
pressing of the coconut flesh alone, without added
water; the second pressing is sold as coconut milk.
Available in cans and cartons from supermarkets.
desiccated concentrated, dried, unsweetened
and finely shredded coconut flesh.
flaked dried flaked coconut flesh.
shredded unsweetened thin strips of dried coconut.
coriander, fresh also called cilantro; bright-
green-leafed herb with a pungent flavour.
cornflakes, gluten-free available from health food
stores or the health food section in supermarkets.
cornflour (corn) also called cornstarch; used as
a thickener. Available made from corn or wheat.
cream of tartar acid ingredient in baking powder;
used in confectionery mixtures to help prevent
sugar from crystallising.
cream we use fresh pouring cream (pure cream).
sour thick, commercially-cultured sour cream with
at least 35% fat content.
thickened a whipping cream containing thickener.
Has at least 35% fat content.

cumin also called zeera or comino; has a spicy, nutty flavour. Available in seed, dried and ground form.

currants dried tiny, almost black raisins so-named from the grape type native to Corinth, Greece.

dates fruit of the date palm tree, eaten fresh or dried. About 4cm to 6cm in length, oval and plump; honey-sweet in flavour with a sticky texture.

dill used fresh or dried, as seeds or ground. Its feathery, frond-like fresh leaves are grassier and more subtle than the dried version or the seeds. Has an anise/celery sweetness.

dried cranberries dried sweetened cranberries.

eggs if a recipe calls for raw or barely cooked eggs, exercise caution if there is a salmonella problem in your area.

flour

bread mix, gluten-free a commercial gluten-free bread mix available from most supermarkets.

buckwheat not a true cereal, but flour is made from its seeds. Available from health food stores.

chickpea also called besan or gram; made from ground chickpeas so is gluten-free and high in protein. Available from health food stores and the health food section in most supermarkets.

plain all-purpose flour made from wheat. Also available gluten-free from most supermarkets.

potato made from cooked potatoes which have been dried and ground.

rice very fine, almost powdery, gluten-free flour; made from ground white rice.

self-raising plain flour mixed with baking powder in the proportion of 1 cup flour to 2 teaspoons baking powder. Also available gluten-free from most supermarkets.

soya flour made from ground soya beans.

food colouring vegetable-based substance available in liquid, paste or gel form.

garam masala literally meaning blended spices; based on varying proportions of cardamom, cinnamon, cloves, coriander, fennel and cumin, roasted and ground together.

gelatine we use powdered gelatine. It is also available in sheet form known as leaf gelatine.

glacé fruit (cherries, pineapple) when buying glacé fruit check the ingredients label for 'glucose made from wheat' – glacé fruit is available without glucose, making it gluten-free and wheat-free.

glacé ginger fresh ginger root preserved in sugar syrup; crystallised ginger can be substituted if rinsed with warm water and dried before use.

golden syrup a by-product of refined sugarcane.

hazelnut meal hazelnuts ground to a coarse flour.

kumara the polynesian name of an orange-fleshed sweet potato often confused with yam.

linseed meal ground linseed (flax seeds). Available from health food stores and in the health food section at some supermarkets.

linseed, sunflower and almond meal (LSA) available from health food stores and in the health food section at some supermarkets.

macadamias a rich, buttery nut. Has a high oil content so should be stored in the refrigerator.

mandarin also called tangerine; a small, loose-skinned, easy-to-peel, sweet and juicy citrus fruit. Mandarin juice is available in the refrigerated section in most supermarkets.

milk we use full-cream milk.

sweetened condensed a canned milk product; milk with more than half its water content removed and sugar added to the milk that remains.

mixed peel candied citrus peel.

mixed spice a blend of ground spices usually consisting of cinnamon, allspice and nutmeg.

noodles, rice vermicelli also called sen mee, mei fun or bee hoon; used in spring rolls and salads. Before using, soak dried noodles in hot water until softened, boil briefly then rinse with hot water.

nutmeg the dried nut of a tree native to Indonesia; available ground or you can grate you own.

oil

cooking spray we use cholesterol-free canola oil.

hazelnut a mono-unsaturated oil, extracted from crushed hazelnuts.

macadamia pressed from ground macadamias. Available in some supermarkets and delicatessens.

vegetable oils from plant rather than animal fats.

onion

green also called scallion or (incorrectly) shallot; an immature onion picked before the bulb has formed, having a long, bright-green edible stalk.

red also called spanish, red spanish or bermuda onion; a sweet-flavoured, large, purple-red onion.

pancetta an Italian unsmoked bacon; pork belly cured in salt and spices then rolled into a sausage shape and dried for several weeks.

pecans golden brown, buttery, rich nut; walnuts are a good substitute. Also available in pieces.

pistachios green, delicately flavoured nuts inside hard off-white shells. Available salted or unsalted in their shells; you can buy them shelled.

polenta also called cornmeal; a flour-like cereal made of corn (maize). Also the dish made from it.

poppy seeds small, dried, bluish-grey seeds; crunchy and nutty. Available whole or ground from delicatessens and most supermarkets.

pure maple syrup distilled from the sap of maple trees. Maple-flavoured syrup or pancake syrup is not an adequate substitute for the real thing.

rice flakes, gluten-free available from the health food section in most supermarkets.

rice, rolled flattened rice grain rolled into flakes; looks similar to rolled oats.

spinach also called english spinach and incorrectly, silver beet. Baby spinach leaves are best eaten raw in salads; the larger leaves can be cooked, but only until barely wilted.

sugar

brown an extremely soft, finely granulated sugar retaining molasses for its colour and flavour.

caster also called superfine or finely granulated table sugar. The fine crystals dissolve easily.

pure icing also known as confectioners' sugar or powdered sugar.

white a coarse, granulated table sugar, also called crystal sugar.

turmeric also called kamin; a rhizome related to galangal and ginger. Must be grated or pounded to release its pungent flavour. Fresh turmeric can be substituted with the more common dried powder.

vanilla

bean dried, long, thin pod from a tropical golden orchid; the minuscule black seeds inside the bean are used to impart a luscious vanilla flavour.

extract obtained from vanilla beans infused in water; a non-alcoholic version of essence.

watercress a peppery salad green; highly perishable, use as soon as possible after purchase.

yogurt we use plain full-cream yogurt unless stated otherwise.

zucchini also called courgette.

conversion chart

measures

One Australian metric measuring cup holds approximately 250ml; one Australian metric tablespoon holds 20ml; one Australian metric teaspoon holds 5ml.

The difference between one country's measuring cups and another's is within a two- or three-teaspoon variance, and will not affect your cooking results. North America, New Zealand and the United Kingdom use a 15ml tablespoon.

All cup and spoon measurements are level. The most accurate way of measuring dry ingredients is to weigh them. When measuring liquids, use a clear glass or plastic jug with the metric markings.

We use large eggs with an average weight of 60g.

dry measures

METRIC	IMPERIAL
15g	½oz
30g	1oz
60g	2oz
90g	3oz
125g	4oz (¼lb)
155g	5oz
185g	6oz
220g	7oz
250g	8oz (½lb)
280g	9oz
315g	10oz
345g	11oz
375g	12oz (¾lb)
410g	13oz
440g	14oz
470g	15oz
500g	16oz (1lb)
750g	24oz (1½lb)
1kg	32oz (2lb)

liquid measures

METRIC	IMPERIAL
30ml	1 fluid oz
60ml	2 fluid oz
100ml	3 fluid oz
125ml	4 fluid oz
150ml	5 fluid oz (¼ pint/1 gill)
190ml	6 fluid oz
250ml	8 fluid oz
300ml	10 fluid oz (½ pint)
500ml	16 fluid oz
600ml	20 fluid oz (1 pint)
1000ml (1 litre)	1¾ pints

length measures

3mm	⅛in
6mm	¼in
1cm	½in
2cm	¾in
2.5cm	1in
5cm	2in
6cm	2½in
8cm	3in
10cm	4in
13cm	5in
15cm	6in
18cm	7in
20cm	8in
23cm	9in
25cm	10in
28cm	11in
30cm	12in (1ft)

oven temperatures

These oven temperatures are only a guide for conventional ovens. For fan-forced ovens, check the manufacturer's manual.

	°C (CELSIUS)	°F (FAHRENHEIT)	GAS MARK
Very slow	120	250	½
Slow	150	275-300	1-2
Moderately slow	160	325	3
Moderate	180	350-375	4-5
Moderately hot	200	400	6
Hot	220	425-450	7-8
Very hot	240	475	9

index

General manager Christine Whiston
Editorial director Susan Tomnay
Creative director Hieu Chi Nguyen
Senior editor Stephanie Kistner
Art director Hannah Blackmore
Introduction Jane Worthington
Food director Pamela Clark
Test Kitchen manager + nutritional information Belinda Farlow
Food editor Caroline Jones
Recipe consultant Cathie Lonnie
Recipe development Nicole Jennings, Rebecca Squadrito
Director of sales Brian Cearnes
Marketing manager Bridget Cody
Marketing & promotions assistant Xanthe Roberts
Senior business analyst Rebecca Varela
Operations manager David Scotto
Production manager Victoria Jefferys
European rights enquiries Laura Bamford lbamford@acpuk.com

acp books

ACP Books are published by ACP Magazines, a division of PBL Media Pty Limited
Publishing director, Women's lifestyle Pat Ingram
Director of sales, Women's lifestyle Lynette Phillips
Commercial manager, Women's lifestyle Seymour Cohen
Marketing director, Women's lifestyle Matthew Dominello
Public relations manager, Women's lifestyle Hannah Deveraux
Research director, Women's lifestyle Justin Stone
PBL Media, Chief Executive Officer Ian Law

Produced by ACP Books, Sydney.
Published by ACP Books, a division of ACP Magazines Ltd, 54 Park St, Sydney; GPO Box 4088, Sydney, NSW 2001
phone (02) 9282 8618 fax (02) 9267 9438 www.acpbooks.com.au
Printed by SNP Leefung, China.
Australia Distributed by Network Services, phone +61 2 9282 8777 fax +61 2 9264 3278 networkweb@networkservicescompany.com.au
United Kingdom Distributed by Australian Consolidated Press (UK), phone (01604) 642 200 fax (01604) 642 300 books@acpuk.com
New Zealand Distributed by Southern Publisher's Group, phone (64 9) 360 0692 fax (64 9) 360 0695 hub@spg.co.nz
South Africa Distributed by PSD Promotions, phone (27 11) 392 6065/6/7 fax (27 11) 392 6079/80 orders@psdprom.co.za
Canada Distributed by Publishers Group Canada, phone (800) 663 5714 fax (800) 565 3770 service@raincoast.com
Title: The Gluten-free Cookbook : Australian women's weekly / food director Pamela Clark.
ISBN: 978-1-86396-745-7 (pbk.)
Notes: Includes index.
Subjects: Gluten-free diet – Recipes.
Other Authors/Contributors: Clark, Pamela.
Also Titled: Australian women's weekly.
Dewey: 641.5638
© ACP Magazines Ltd 2009
ABN 18 053 273 546
This publication is copyright. No part of it may be reproduced or transmitted in any
form without the written permission of the publishers.

The publishers would like to thank the following for props used in photography:
Ici et la; Mint Condition Recycled Clothes; Spotlight; Annabel Trends; Maxwell & Williams; Lantern Studios; Rhubarb;
Paper Couture; Oxford Art Supplies; No Chintz; St Vincent de Paul Society Store; Radford Furnishings;
Funkis Swedish Forms; Royal Doulton; Rapee; French Bull; Dandi; Fabric Deli; Salvos Stores.

Cover Chocolate strawberry tart, page 89
Photographer Teny Aghamalian **Stylist** Louise Bickle **Food preparation** Amal Webster

To order books, phone 136 116 (within Australia) or
online at www.acpbooks.com.au
Send recipe enquiries to:
recipeenquiries@acpmagazines.com.au